WEEDS, ROADS, AND GOD

A Half-Century of Culture Change
among the Philippine Ga'dang

BEN J. WALLACE
Southern Methodist University

WAVELAND

PRESS, INC.

Long Grove, Illinois

For information about this book, contact:
    Waveland Press, Inc.
    4180 IL Route 83, Suite 101
    Long Grove, IL 60047-9580
    (847) 634-0081
    info@waveland.com
    www.waveland.com

In memory of my friend Lidjou Dubadob
and for the younger generation of Ga'dang
whose culture, both past and present,
I have tried to preserve in this book.

Contents

Preface

*A*ny book that covers ethnographic research by the same investigator separated by a time gap of almost 50 years will be highly personal. This is the case here and I make no apology for personalizing the presentation. To do any less would diminish the value of studies of culture change, and it would deny the reader the opportunity to examine my biases as an ethnographer, in the past and the present. The book not only reflects culture change among a group of people I studied in 1965–66 and restudied 45 years later, but also it is a general indicator of changes among similar cultures in the northern Philippines. I examine environmental, social, and culture changes as illustrated by the Ga'dang of the Philippines, changes in my personal approach to fieldwork, and to a lesser degree, changes in the field of ethnographic research and writing.

The 1960s, the decade of my original Ga'dang study, was a period of dramatic social change in the United States, as well as change in anthropology. By 1965, the Vietnam War was worsening, and with the bombing of North Vietnam, increasing numbers of war deaths were recorded. Riots took place in the South Central Los Angeles neighborhood of Watts. Betty Friedan and Gloria Steinem ushered in the women's liberation movement in 1963, and John F. Kennedy was assassinated that same year, followed by the assassination of Malcolm X in 1965, and Martin Luther King and Robert F. Kennedy in 1968. On college campuses, the baby boomer students joined with faculty and others to protest the Vietnam War. On a lighter note, during the 1960s, Ken Kesey's *One Flew Over the Cuckoo's Nest* became a best-selling novel, Elvis returned from the U.S. Army to the stage, and the Beatles were booed as they departed Manila with "Beatles *alis dayan!*" (Go home Beatles!). In 1966, Timothy Leary promoted the use of LSD, the hippie rock musical *Hair* was a hit on Broadway, and men wore colorful polyester pants as they escorted women with bouffant hairstyles to see the blockbuster movies *Midnight Cowboy* and *The Graduate.*

Changes in ethnographic theories, methods, and ethics during the 1960s were academically no less dramatic than the general societal changes that were emerging during that decade. What some scholars called the new ethnography or ethnoscience reached its intellectual peak in the 1960s along with the emic/etic debate in anthropological linguistics. The formalist and the substantive debate in economic anthropology flourished during this decade. The ecological model for ethnographic research became a popular and productive approach to understand society and culture. The 1960s also witnessed the refinement and validation of gender studies, Marxist anthropology, symbolic anthropology, urban anthropology, and medical anthropology. The standard fieldwork guide of *Notes and Queries on Anthropology* (1951), while still valuable as a guide to fieldwork in the 1960s, was being augmented by a myriad of promising ideas, theories, and methods from the newer and developing fields in anthropology. It was these new and sometimes underdeveloped, sometimes contradictory, concepts that young ethnographers carried with them into the field setting during the 1960s. These fieldworkers also carried with them a new awareness of anthropological ethics, especially as related to U.S. government interactions throughout the world.

A further challenge for many fieldworkers of the 1960s was the expectation that we would find waiting for us groups of people that reflected so-called primitive cultures as described in George Peter Murdock's *Our Primitive Contemporaries* (1934) or Elman Service's *A Profile of Primitive Culture* (1958), both of which were used as undergraduate textbooks in world ethnology courses. Occasionally, we found such peoples, often geographically isolated, some practicing technologies carried over from earlier centuries, nonliterate, and maintaining much of their traditional culture. More often, and to our surprise, we found that many of these peoples were under intense culture stress because of their more dominant cultural neighbors, and that they were forced to confront the influences of modernizing nation-states. The societies were not so isolated as we had been led to believe. We found that our ethnographic observations had to be analyzed within the context of cultures in the process of change, often in the process of cultural disintegration. The traditional subject of ethnology, the so-called "primitive society," was vanishing. Many of us recognized that we were witnessing a way of life that was disappearing from the globe, never to reappear. We knew that the days of the "bush" anthropologist were limited.

The people and places in this book are real, only the names of people have been changed. The Ga'dang area is sufficiently small enough that to strive for anonymity of location would serve no purpose.

Since almost 50 years passed between my original Ga'dang study and my restudy, many colleagues and students helped me to understand better what it is to be an ethnographer. I am deeply indebted to all, and I extend to them my sincere appreciation. In particular, I want to thank the many Ga'dang I have known, living and dead, who have helped me. Without their aid, I could not have completed the original study or the restudy. For help during the restudy, I also want to express my appreciation to the *sitio, barangay,* and municipal officials of Paracelis, Mountain Province, for providing me with some statistical and map data that would have been difficult to obtain without their help.

For funding and/or housing and logistical support specifically related to the Ga'dang research in the past and the present, I am indebted to the Midwest Universities Consortium for International Activities; the University of Wisconsin, Madison; the Agricultural Development Council, Inc.; Ateneo de Manila; University of the Philippines College of Agriculture, Los Baños; the University of California, Santa Barbara; the Wenner Gren Foundation; Southern Methodist University; Caltex, Philippines; the Plum Foundation; and the Green Earth Legacy Foundation, Inc.

Ben J. Wallace
Dallas, Texas
2013

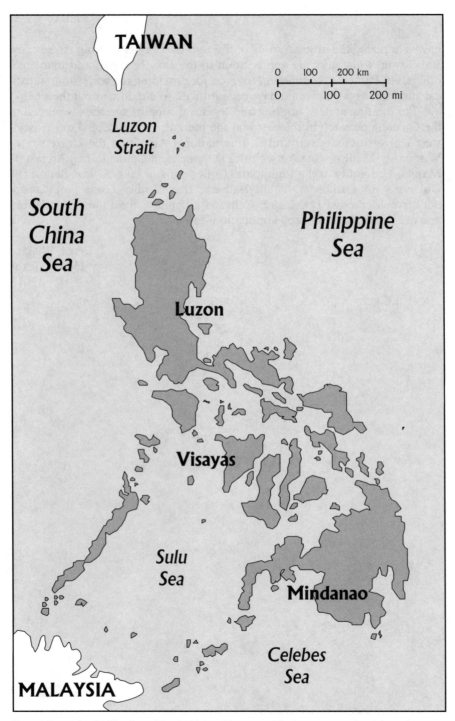

Republic of the Philippines (shaded islands), an archipelago categorized into three geographical divisions: Luzon, Visayas, and Mindanao.

Chapter 1

Introduction

An ethnography is the systematic description and analysis of a society at a point in time, and a place in space. The description and analysis includes cultural variations within the society and the placement of the society as a part of the greater physical and social environment. If the researcher is prepared, is a good observer, and has the capability to analyze what he or she has seen and heard, the ethnography will be a realistic depiction of the community at the time, and in the place, when the ethnographer observed it. As an ethnographic description and analysis, it is a reasonable portrayal of the society as it existed a few years before, and a few years after, the ethnographer lived with and studied the people. By anthropological tradition, to reach this level of understanding, the ethnographer learns the local language and lives with a particular people for a continuous period of 12 months or longer. This is done mainly to insure that the full yearly cycle of cultural events are observed and as a means of witnessing the complex interactions of cultural similarities and differences that bind and thread together the components of the society. This initiation ritual for becoming an ethnographer remains the standard by which ethnographic research is judged today for those researchers who respect and value the ethnographic traditions of our predecessors. Living in the field was the customary practice of distinguished anthropologists in the days of Franz Boas (1888), the approach of early twentieth-century pioneers such as Margaret Mead (1928) and Bronislaw Malinowski (1984[1922]), as well as of later twentieth-century ethnographers like Laura Bohannan (1954), Harold Conklin (1957), and Roy Rappaport (2000[1984]).

Studying Social and Culture Change

Fredrik Barth (1967:661) reminded anthropology more than 40 years ago, "To understand social change, what we need to do as social anthropologists is to describe all of society in such terms that we see how it persists,

1

maintains itself, and changes through time." Barth's comments are as germane today as they were in 1967. The central themes here are "all of society," "how it persists," "maintains itself," and "through time." My focus is to address the issue of "changes through time" as expressed among the Ga'dang over a period of 45 years by comparing data from my 1965–66 study (Wallace 1969, 1970) with data gathered in 2010 and 2011. Effectively, this is a comparative ethnography, except the comparison is between time periods within the same culture rather than between cultures.

While the study of social and culture change long has been a major theme of anthropology, and the profession has made advancements in research on change since Barth made his statement, the studies have had limited success, mainly because of the problems associated with establishing a baseline from which to measure social and culture change. Often, the baseline from which change is measured is dependent on ethnographic reconstruction (e.g., Benedict 1934; Honigmann 1963; Perry 1983; Steward 1936; and Wallace 1964) and the use of the concept of the ethnographic present (Halstead et al. 2008; Sanjek 1991). Ethnographic reconstruction involves synthesizing information based on the memory of explorers, elderly informants remembering their youth and what their parents told them, and the use of other techniques in historiography that are too often laden with a wide range of interpretations (Bentley 1999).

Restudies of ethnographic situations by an anthropologist of the work of an earlier anthropologist have helped the profession to understand better the process of culture change, but they also have further complicated the issue of studying culture change. Like research based on ethnographic reconstruction, these types of restudies are not without inherent difficulties. Three well-known and controversial examples will suffice as an illustration: the ethnography of the Trobriand Islanders by Bronislaw Malinowski (1984[1922]) and the later study of the Trobriand Islanders by Annette Weiner (1976), Margaret Mead's (1928) study of Samoan culture as compared to Derek Freeman's (1983) later study of Samoan culture, and Oscar Lewis' (1951) study of the Mexican village of Tepotzlan, which Robert Redfield (1930) had studied almost 20 years earlier.

Malinowski did his fieldwork in the Trobriand Islands during 1915–1918. His famous *Argonauts of the Western Pacific* was first published in 1922. Weiner's study, culminating in her *Women of Value, Men of Renown: New Perspectives in Trobriand Exchange* (1976) was conducted in the Trobriand Islands almost 60 years after Malinowski. A reading of these two ethnographies clearly demonstrates that the Trobriand Islanders of Weiner's study are markedly different from the Trobriand Islanders of Malinowski's study, especially with regard to trade, the work of women, and wealth. How much of this difference is due to an interpretation of Trobriand Island culture based on the gender and cultural background of the researcher, the time period of the study, and the methodological and theoretical orientation of the researcher (Jolly 1992; Tuzin 1997), and how much of the difference is due to Trobriand Island culture change, remains unclear.

Mead, in the book that launched her illustrious career, *Coming of Age in Samoa* (1928), describes a society where personal confrontations are few in number, where life is idyllic, and sex is available just for the asking and finding a secluded place. Conversely, Freeman, who spent many years researching Samoan culture, in his *Margaret Mead and Samoa: The Making and Unmaking of an Anthropological Myth* (1983), notes that some of Mead's observations, especially about Samoan character and sex, were misunderstood by her or that she was purposely misled by some Samoans (Holmes 1987; Orans 1996). At best, Freeman accuses Mead of incompetence, and at worst, of academic fraud. The issues dividing these two scholars may never be resolved to the satisfaction of their supporters. The differences, however, clearly demonstrate some of the problems associated with restudies not conducted by the original ethnographers.

Redfield went to the Mexican village of Tepotzlan in 1926, and his *Tepotzlan, a Mexican Village* was published in 1930. In this classic book in anthropology, he describes a harmonious and culturally homogeneous community undergoing a smooth transition into a modernizing Mexico. In 1943, Lewis initiated his restudy of Tepotzlan, the results of which were published as *Life in a Mexican Village: Tepotzlan Restudied* (1951). He found this same village, approximately 15 years later, to be culturally heterogeneous, with significant differences in wealth, and stressed with internal power struggles. Are the perceptions of these two scholars of the same village due to their backgrounds (Redfield, the son of a prominent urban attorney, and Lewis, the son of a poor farmer), or to their political orientation? Did Tepotzlan change that much in 15 years, or did one of them misunderstand what he saw and heard (Rigdon 1988)?

Longitudinal studies of the same community have obvious advantages for the study of culture change, most notably there is a known baseline and there is continuous monitoring of the changes in the culture. The value of longitudinal studies is clearly illustrated in the most notable of long-term projects: the Tzintzunzan project in Mexico and the Gwembe project in Zambia (see Foster et al. 1979). But, as discussed by Royce and Kemper (2002:xiv–xxxviii), longitudinal studies are not without issues that have to be considered, especially in the areas of defining multigenerational core data and dealing with the issue of people and households entering and leaving the community. As Royce and Kemper note, "The community is the same, but its membership varies" (2002:xxix). There is no doubt that the potential for learning about change in human society is great in long-term research projects. The question becomes, however, when will these projects end and be summarized?

Restudies of a community by the ethnographer who originally studied the community are not common (see Firth 1959; Guyer 1997; Hart 2004; Knauft 2002; Wilson 1970). This may change in the near future as the many ethnologists who received their PhD in the late 1960s and the early 1970s are approaching retirement. These scholars are in a good position to do a restudy using data from their first major work as a cultural baseline (see Kehoe et al.

2010). Why the number of restudies by the original ethnographer is sparse is unclear. Perhaps it is because as we mature professionally, we develop other interests, geographically or theoretically; opportunities present themselves to work elsewhere; or we are limited in the time available to us because of teaching and administrative responsibilities. In my case, my research took me in a more applied direction, so I was afforded opportunities to do research in other regions. Since the bulk of my research continued to be in Asia, however, I was often back in the Philippines, so I was able to return to the Ga'dang from time to time—not to restudy them, but to visit old friends.

My aim here is to present an analysis of culture change among the Ga'dang of the mountains of the Philippines by integrating the more structured or scientific approach of the social sciences with the less structured postmodernist or interpretive approach of the narrative and the humanities (cf. Geertz 1973; Jenkins 1997; Lett 1997; Ortner 1984; Spiro 1996; Zeitlyn 2009). The so-called scientific and the interpretive approaches differ significantly for theoretical extremists, but as used here, the epistemological and ideological differences between the two views are resolvable, especially because the aim is to depict culture change among the same group of people over a period of almost a half-century.

While I consider what the anthropologist Margery Wolf (1992:1) calls "postmodernist ruminations," in her balanced examination of feminism, fieldwork, and postmodernism, I am equally concerned with applying the theme posited by the eminent ecologist Paul Sears (1939:127) of "What is happening in nature?" to the study of culture change and ethnographic research. Wolf offers three texts that describe what happened in the village of Peihotien—fiction written by Wolf, unanalyzed field notes written by members of the field staff, and a narrative of observations and interviews written by Wolf. "In each can be found examples of attitudes, methods, and ideas that our postmodern critics both hate and love" (Wolf 1992:7). Sears (1939), despite the complexity of studying an ecological system—the interrelationship between organisms and their environment—posits that, fundamentally the question being asked is straightforward: "What is happening in nature?" I am asking this question as it relates to what is happening among the Ga'dang in the environment in which they live.

In this book, while acknowledging some of the critiques of the postmodernists, I focus on what has happened environmentally, economically, socially, and spiritually among the Ga'dang of the Philippines over a 45-year period. My approach to restudying the Ga'dang has been one of focusing on measurable empirical data while recognizing that some of my observations are interpretive. I make no claim that the study is as scientific as I would prefer, nor that it can be replicated in another 50 years, but the study is far more than a "genre of storytelling" (Bruner 1986:139) as certain writers would have the profession believe of some ethnographies.

It is generally agreed within anthropology that ethnographic research is fundamentally reflexive, that is, the researcher is aware of how a variety of factors, such as his or her position in the culture, concept of self within the field setting, theoretical framework within which he or she is working, and so forth, affect the research (Davies 1999:87; Robertson 2002; Salzman 2002). Nevertheless, the extent to which reflexivity affects ethnographic analysis remains an open question. My experience suggests that reflexivity in ethnology can be managed, and observing a similar event with the same eyes in much the same way over time is possible. What complicates the situation is that ethnographers must now deal with a wealth of conflicting popular and professional publications and opinions, which reflect how cultures and societies have changed, while at the same time maintaining a balance between the demands of science and a consciousness of self.

Jaarsma and Rohatynskyj (2000) argue that ethnography is in trouble because of globalization. There is in the profession what they call a crisis of representation, where the subjects of ethnography are now demanding accountability. This crisis is "set in motion by rapid social and economic changes in a globalized world" (2000:1). Nancy Scheper-Hughes (2001, originally published in 1979), addresses this challenge. She contributes to an understanding of the issue of accountability when she discusses the "difficulties of balancing one's responsibilities to honest ethnography with care and respect for the people who shared a part of their lives and their secrets with me" (2001:xiii). Her concerns for the balance between honest ethnography done with care and respect for the community are made clear when she reiterates, perhaps with a little candid remorse, that she had asked forgiveness of the villagers in her original study for "exposing the darker and weaker side of their venerable culture" (2001:xxi), knowing that forgiveness would not be forthcoming. Scheper-Hughes had the daring to express in writing what other ethnographers have only considered.

If, as Jaarsma and Rohatynskyj (2000) argue, there is a crisis of representation in ethnology because of globalism, then ethnographers should welcome this "crisis." The crisis gives ethnology the opportunity to communicate with both public and academic audiences, refine its methods and analytical tools, and address the issues of social and culture change—a priority for anthropology from its beginning, but never fully dealt with to the satisfaction of the profession. Importantly, as cogently argued by Amselle (2002), even the most isolated societies have always been a part of a wider network of societies. Anthropology should be less concerned with the distinction between the so-called isolation of "primitive" societies and the pervasiveness of "modern" societies and focus on cultural comparisons and the processes of culture diffusion (cf. Amselle 2002), or examine the processes that bring the descendants of the "primitive" societies into the "modern" world. The argument that change is due to "globalism" avoids the issue.

To even the most casual observer, it is clear that the so-called gimme caps (baseball-style caps embroidered or stamped with the logo of the organization that hands them out for free) and T-shirts displaying various advertisements have become a cultural homogenizer in many parts of the world.

Despite some thoughtful attempts to deal with the concept of globalization (see Amselle 2002; Eriksen 2003, 2007; Inda and Rosaldo 2007; and Lewellen 2002), it would appear that "globalism" has been used as an explanation for social change more than as a way to understand the complex process conditioning social change. Between the years 2000 and 2010, 107 articles appeared with "global" in the title in 63 of the major journals in anthropology (see www.jstor.org). If reviews are included from these journals, the number of times "global" appeared increases to 254.

In these journals the range of topics covered by the umbrella of globalism is immense: dying, capitalism, feminism, healing, hip-hop, human rights, human organs, race, high heels, supermarkets, antigender, language, folklore, popular culture, kinship, and fiction, to mention only a few. It would appear that instead of responding to globalization with methods and modes of analyses to understand the processes involved in culture change, the profession has answered with an inventory of what is happening in the modern world, and with "isms" such as postmodernism, poststructuralism, and neo-liberalism.

One way to appreciate the processes of culture change is for ethnographers to restudy the communities they studied in the past. Accountability issues from the past and the present can be compared by the original researcher, eliminating the problems that occur when a different set of eyes and ears does a subsequent study. In addition, the younger subjects of an earlier ethnography, many of whom are now literate, can more easily question and critique—demand accountability from the ethnographer of the original study and the restudy. It should be noted, however, that just because these younger and literate observers are examining their own culture or reading about their culture, their interpretations are seldom more insightful than the observations of a trained, honest, and sensitive ethnographer. For example, a committed "born-again Christian" Ga'dang is very likely to view the changes in his culture much differently than a Ga'dang who goes to the Christian church occasionally, or has attended college.

Replicating studies involving human behavior, especially in the field setting, is challenging. Maintaining an awareness of the problems associated with restudies and a consistency in observation by the same ethnographer, however, is a realistic activity. As an ethnographer, I can measure and count trees, land, and people the same way I did 30 years ago; I can record linguistic terms and concepts the same way I did 40 years ago; and I can observe and describe a ritual using the same terminology I used 50 years ago. Does this mean that an ethnographic restudy I might do now of the people I studied almost a half-century ago is replicated? Certainly not: I have changed and the people have changed. In addition, even in the smaller and more isolated cultures there is variation in cultural knowledge and in behavior. Nevertheless, one of the best opportunities for the profession to understand the process of culture change is for ethnographers to restudy the same culture they studied years before.

In 2010, I took leave from a development project and initiated a restudy of the Ga'dang. I had planned to wait until the 50th year for the restudy, but two of my oldest Ga'dang friends died within a year of one another, so I decided it was time to get started. The study is not based on a re-created baseline; change is measured against my field notes and experiences from 1965 and 1966 when I first lived with the Ga'dang, and a brief revisit in 1968 (Wallace 1969, 1970). It is not a longitudinal study, as it was not done until 45 years after I first did the study. It is a restudy of a group of people done by the original ethnographer almost one-half century later. Despite the cynicism that many years in the academy tends to foster, by waiting 45 years to do the restudy, hopefully I bring some maturity, some experience, and some new insight to understanding the processes of culture change. My worldview has changed over these many years, but my core self is much the same. My strengths and weaknesses, my biases and objectivity, as an ethnographer have not changed dramatically. The lenses through which I view the Ga'dang today are much the same as when I first witnessed their culture almost 50 years ago, although my hope is that the lenses now are tinted with experience and greater clarity.

The Ga'dang and the Gaddang

Linguistically, there has long been confusion in the popular and scientific literature regarding the ethnic group or groups called the "Gaddang." There are in fact at least four closely related Gaddang languages in Northern Luzon (Luzon is the largest island in the Philippines) (see Lewis 2009). The people of this restudy are the Ga'dang. As spoken, Ga'dang, with a distinct glottal stop between the "a" and the "d," identifies them as a particular group of people—Ga'dang—who speak a common language. These mountain people prefer "Ga'dang" as an identifier of them as a group and as a people who speak a common language. In spoken Ga'dang, the term "gaddang" has a meaning of its own. Popular beliefs among non-Ga'dang speakers is that "gaddang" means carabao (water buffalo), referring to the Ga'dang being darker in skin color than many other groups in the Cordillera Central. While many Ga'dang joke about being darker than their neighbors, when I asked Ga'dang from Mountain Province for the meaning of "gaddang," I was told that it means "skin," and nothing more. It should be noted, the term "Gaddang" is the designation that has been used since the arrival of the Spanish, and it has been established in both the popular and academic literature. Importantly, however, in written usage—in English, Ilocano (the language spoken by the dominant ethnic group of the same name), or other languages—educated Ga'dang spell Ga'dang as Gaddang, suggesting that whether or not to use Ga'dang or Gaddang may be more a concern of scholars than of the local people.

In 1965, the Gaddang and the Ga'dang inhabited the northern part of the province of Nueva Vizcaya, sections of the province of Isabela, and the eastern parts of the provinces of Ifugao and Bontoc (now called Mountain Province). Today, the Gaddang still live in Nueva Vizcaya and nearby provinces, but the bulk of the Ga'dang who were the subjects of the 1965–66 study now live in Ifugao and Mountain Province. There are no longer Ga'dang living in the forested pockets of Isabela because there are very few forested areas in western Isabela. In the past, the "Gaddang" could easily be divided into two groups: the Pagan Gaddang and the Christian Gaddang. This is no longer the situation. Because of the changes in culture over the past 50 years, the terminology depicting the different groups of "Gaddang" has been modified.

The "Gaddang" who were traditionally identified as the Christian Gaddang (Galang 1935; Lambrecht 1959, 1960; Lumicao-Lormaa 1984) are Lowland Gaddang. Numbering around 30,000, this includes the native inhabitants of northern Nueva Vizcaya—in the towns of Bayombong, Solano, and Bagabag—and some of groups scattered throughout Isabela. It would also include the Gaddang speakers of the Santiago-Echague area who still identify themselves as Yogad, and the Gaddang speakers of Angadanan, Cayuayan, and Reyna Merecedes who still call themselves Cagayano.

According to some Ga'dang with whom I discussed the issue of culture change, there may be a few very old individuals in the remote areas of the mountain municipality of Paracelis, Mountain Province, who are living a more traditional lifestyle, but in general, there are no non-Christian Ga'dang today. All Ga'dang now follow, to a lesser or greater degree of syncretism, some form of Christianity. In the 1960s, many small communities of Ga'dang maintained a culture of their own, not having significantly adopted the ways of the lowland Filipino (lowlander). They easily could be identified visually by their clothing and housing. Today, except for some of the women who wear a few traditional beads, it is not easy to distinguish visually a Ga'dang from any other Filipino living in the area. Fifty years ago, the Ga'dang, as viewed by the Christian Gaddang and other lowlanders, often were not Ga'dang: they were "Kalinga." Many lowlanders perceived the Ga'dang—whom they often called Kalinga—to be dangerous headhunters who lived in the mountain forests. Often, the Ga'dang promoted this image. It served as a mechanism to protect them and their lands from the ever-increasing number of encroaching lowlanders, which characterized the 1960s.

Because of the changes in culture and because of the ways other populations now perceive the Ga'dang, currently it is more accurate to divide the Gaddang into two major groups: the Ga'dang, the majority of whom occupy the greater Paracelis area, and the northeastern parts of Ifugao, and the Lowland Gaddang, who formally were known as the Christian Gaddang. Unless otherwise noted, throughout this book, I use the term "Ga'dang" to refer to the Ga'dang living along the lower eastern slopes of the Cordillera Central. These are the same people, along with their descendents, who in the 1960s were called "Pagan Gaddang" and were the subjects of my 1965–66 study.

The history of the Gaddang is reasonably well documented (see Aduarte 1640; Beyer 1917; Blair and Robertson 1907; Keesing 1962; Landor 1904; Malumbres 1918; NCCR 2000). When the Gaddang first were identified at the beginning of the seventeenth century by the Spanish as "Gaddanes," they were scattered in and around the forests of the middle and upper Cagayan area, mainly to the west of the Magat River, and extending up the Cordillera, roughly the same territory they occupied during the 1960s, the time period of my original study.

Of the Gaddang, a seventeenth-century Spanish observer said:

> This tribe was always regarded as one on a lower plane of civilization than the others, and more devoted to freedom, enemies to subjection; for they were a race in the most distant mountains and wilderness of that province, and they had less communication and commerce than did the other tribes—not only with the Spanish, but even with the rest of the Indians. (Aduarte 1640:113)

The Gaddang initially resisted the Spanish and acted as the principals in at least one insurrection against the Spanish. This 1621 revolt, as described by a Spanish observer, follows:

> The insurgents immediately began to commit a thousand extravagances. They set fire to the houses, they drank and they annoyed the people in the village. If any were unwilling to join them, they threatened them with death by holding lances at their breasts. The result was that many joined them, being forced by fear of instant death, and waiting for a better time when they could again have religion. A few of them succeeded in hiding and going down the river after the father. . . . The insurgents did not cease until they had aroused all the villages in the vicinity. As men abandoned of God, and directed by the devil, they were guilty of horrible sacrileges [slashing the church image and misusing other sacred objects] . . . as a barbarous tribe of apostates. (Keesing 1962:252)

Within a year, the rebellion was suppressed by the Spanish, and some of the Gaddang began to accept the Christian teaching of the Spanish friars. By the mid-1700s, large numbers of Gaddang had become Christians. In 1740, for example, one priest (Blair and Robertson 1907:130) reports "six hundred persons came to enroll themselves for the catechism from the Yogad and Gaddang tribes." By 1900, almost all Gaddang were Christianized (Beyer 1917; Landor 1904). As Keesing (1962:336) noted for the 1960s, "Those 'infidels' who were not converted and resettled earlier came within the spheres of governmental and mission influence in the latter nineteenth and early twentieth centuries, so that by today only small pockets of non-Christians remain in the least accessible strongholds." My original Ga'dang study was among these small pockets of non-Christian Ga'dang.

Two such pockets of non-Christian Ga'dang, the settlements of Cabanuangan and Pakak, served as the focus of my original 1965–66 study. The Ga'dang at Pakak practiced shifting or swidden cultivation (*uma* in Ga'dang and *kaingin* in other areas). The Ga'dang at Cabanuangan used the water buffalo (carabao) as draft animals and the plow for tilling the soil. Only ten years earlier, both groups of Ga'dang lived in the same village in a nearby forest. With the influx of Ilocano and others, the forest was depleted and no longer suitable for uma cultivation. At the time, these Ga'dang and other Ga'dang settlements located farther west into the mountains could be considered relics of a Philippine ethnic group, with a distinctively non-Christian culture; hence, the common use of the term Pagan Gaddang at the time.

The Ga'dang: 1965 and 2010

By 1968, the settlement of Pakak no longer existed as described in the 1965–66 study. The forests of Pakak were almost depleted, so the households moved farther into the mountains in order to continue their slash-and burn cultivation way of life, eventually settling closer and closer to the mountain communities of Paracelis, the region they identified as the most culturally "Ga'dang." While the Ga'dang living in Cabanuangan were still culturally non-Christian Ga'dang, they nonetheless had already shifted their farming system to plow agriculture. Some of the Cabanuangan Ga'dang moved with the Pakak Ga'dang farther into the mountains. Other Ga'dang in Cabanuangan chose to remain in the area, effectively abandoning their traditional Ga'dang ways, and married local Cagayanos (people from the province of Cagayon) and Ilocanos. As a distinctive cultural entity, they disappeared.

The Ga'dang who had been living in the pockets of remaining forests in the provinces of Isabela and Ifugao slowly migrated to the southern area of the municipality of Paracelis, Mountain Province. Specifically, some Ga'dang families from my earlier study began to join other Ga'dang families in the village of Bayongyong, located in the *barangay* (district or ward) of Bananao, Paracelis. In the Philippine political structure, a province is composed of several municipalities, usually each municipality is comprised of several barangay, each of which is then divided into several *sitio* (village; sometimes called a *purok*). When I first visited Bayongyong in 1965, it was a very small settlement consisting of only four or five houses (and was not an official Philippine political unit). Thus, the subdivisions of the municipality are:

Province: Mountain Province
Municipality: Paracelis
Several small villages: Bananao
Village: Bayongyong

In 1966, Bananao was a sitio of the barangay of Butigue. At that time, if a party was traveling to the area, either by walking or by poling a boat up the Siffu River, the group was traveling to an area called Butigue. Four years later, Bananao was administratively made into a barangay of the *municipio* of Paracelis. Bayongyong was given sitio status a few years later.

The barangay or community of Bananao, in particular the village or sitio (sometimes two or three sitio comprise a barangay) of Bayongyong, is the focus of this restudy of the Ga'dang. This village was selected for the focus of the restudy because a few elderly people from my 1965–66 study live there, the children of several families from the 1965–66 study live there, and I visited Bayongyong several times during the earlier Ga'dang study, usually by walking there, but occasionally by poling a small boat upriver. The place has changed dramatically, but some of the people are the same, except that they are almost 50 years older than when I first knew them.

Mountain Province is one political unit of what is called the Cordillera Administrative Region, which consists of the provinces of Abra, Apayao, Benguet, Ifugao, Kalinga and Mountain Province. Most of the peoples of these provinces are considered by the government to be minority indigenous tribes, and collectively are labeled the Igorot. The Irogots of these provinces are generally believed to have arrived in the islands sometime between 5000 BC and 2000 BC. Not all researchers agree on dates and paths, but most scholars accept that the first people to arrive in the Philippines were the Aeta (Negrito,) perhaps round 20,000 BC, followed by successive waves or migrations of Austronesian speakers either from the Asian mainland via Formosa or from the southern part of China around 5000 BC and 2000 BC (cf. Beyer 1953; Gaillard and Mallari 2004; Jocano 1975; Scott 1992).

Presently, the Mountain Province municipality of Paracelis (CAR 2010) is classified by the Philippine government as a third-class municipality (there are six classes), suggesting it is typical for a relatively isolated, farming community, with a low population density. The area of Paracelis became an official municipality in 1962 under the name of Paracale, and the name was changed to Paracelis in 1966. Currently, the major populations of Paracelis are Ga'dang, Balangao, Kalinga, and Ilocano. Politically, Paracelis is divided into nine barangay, the *Poblacion* (usually the central barangay of the municipality) housing 5,319 people with an average barangay size of 2,745 people.

Currently, the total population of the barangay of Bananao is 2,207 people living in 416 households (Bananao Census 2010) in five sitio. Forty-four percent of the households in Bananao are Ga'dang (182 households), 30 percent are Balangao (128 households), 20 percent are Ilocano (87 households), and the remaining 6 percent (19 households) are Ifugao and other Mountain Province people. As calculated by local officials, the ethnicity claimed by the head of the house, either man or female, serves as the ethnic designation of the household. Bayongyong, politically a sitio of Bananao, is an all Ga'dang village consisting of 22 households with a total of 126 people. Bayongyong represents 13 percent of the total number of Ga'dang households in Bananao and 13 percent of the Ga'dang population in Bananao. Population statistics for Bananao and Bayongyong are, as follows.

Barangay Bananao

Total Population	2,207
Total Ga'dang	964
Total Households	416
Ga'dang Households	182
Balangao Households	128
Ilocano Households	87
Other Households	19

Sitio Bayongyong

Total Population	126
Number of Households	22

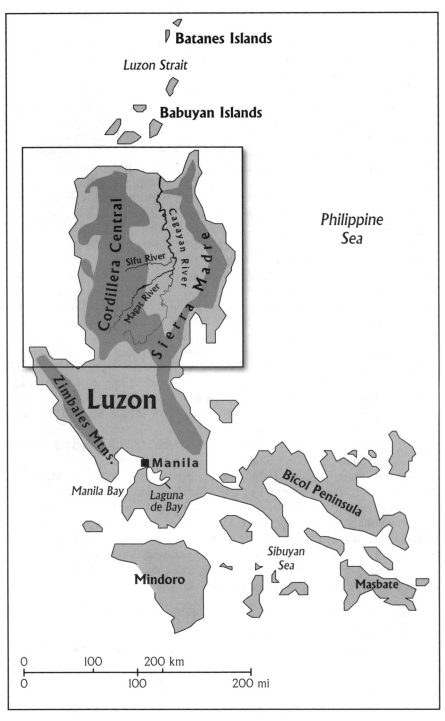

Northern Luzon, as situated within Luzon.

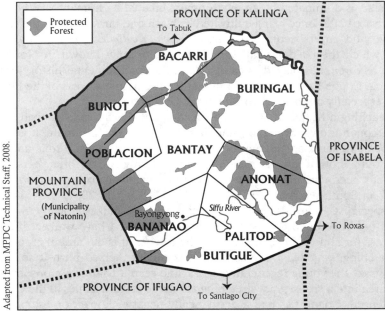

Adapted from MPDC Technical Staff, 2008.

Provinces of Northern Luzon, showing the Cordillera Administrative Region, the Cagayan Valley, and the Municipality of Paracelis, Mountain Province *(top)*. Municipality of Paracelis showing nine barangay *(bottom)*.

Bayongyong and much of the greater Paracelis area are environmentally similar to the rest of the eastern slopes of the Cordillera Central (see Huke 1963; Wernstedt and Spencer 1967). Approximately 83 percent of Mountain Province is mountainous. The houses in Bayongyong are located along or near a winding and mountainous dirt road (constructed in the 1970s and still unpaved) roughly halfway between the Ifugao/Ilocano community of Alfonso Lista (known as Potia during the 1995–66 study) in Ifugao Province and the predominantly Kalinga community of Tabuk in Kalinga Province. The villages of the Paracelis area are generally around 800 to 1,000 feet in elevation, but the mountains to the west range up to 5,000-plus feet. Bayongyong is located along this road (originally a footpath) at the Siffu River in the southern region of Paracelis.

There are two seasons, a short dry season lasting from January through April, and a longer wet season from May through December. The area is subject to a tropical monsoon climate where plants grow continually, provided there is adequate water supply. Thirty-five percent of the typhoons that reach the Philippines strike Northern Luzon, which includes the eastern slopes of the Cordillera Central and the Ga'dang community of Bayongyong. The average rainfall is around 74 inches a year; the wettest month is November and the driest is March.

The area, except for very small patches of primary forest and larger patches of secondary forest cover, usually around a half to one square kilometer in size, is dominated by an environment created by humanity. When left uncultivated after once being cultivated by slash-and-burn or plow, the dominant ground cover becomes the grass *Imperata cylindrica*, (L) Beauv. This grass, which the Ga'dang call *akun* but is commonly known in Northern Luzon as *cogon*, has played a major role in the environmental history of the Ga'dang. Cogon has become a dominant feature of many areas of the Philippines, especially on the eastern side of the Cordillera.

Reaching a height of 80 cm, and having flat, linear, spike-shaped, erect leaves, cogon grows throughout the Paracelis area. When mature, it is often too coarse to serve as grazing for cattle. It thrives in infertile soils and can choke out a crop of rain-fed rice in a matter of only two to three years. This grass has been classified as one of the top ten most noxious and invasive grasses in Southeast Asia (see GISD 2010; MacDonald 2004). As noted by plant specialists, it invades disturbed ecosystems and makes it nearly impossible for other plants to coexist (Chikoye et al. 2002). I have walked through this grass for almost 50 years, been cut by it when it is tall and dry, pulled it for thatching, watched it choke out fields of rice, helped burn it so cattle could graze the young regenerative grass, and seen it change a monsoon forested area into a sea of grass stretching along the eastern slopes of the Cordillera Central. Cogon has had a dramatically negative impact on the peoples and the environment of Isabela, Ifugao, Kalinga, and Mountain Province.

The mountains located to the west of the Bananao are higher than where the Ga'dang villages are located, and there is more primary and secondary forest cover. Except for a few birds, snakes, and lizards, what little animal life exists in the area can be found in these mountains. Although limited in number as compared to 50 years ago, a variety of birds such as doves, pigeons, hornbills, parakeets, and hawks; numerous reptiles; a smattering of Malay civets, long-tailed macaques, and wild boar; and an occasional Sambar deer can be seen in the forests. These animals, however, are not sufficient in numbers to contribute to the Ga'dang diet or economy.

The author with Ga'dang in Bananao, 1965 *(top)*.
The author with Ga'dang in Bananao, 2010 *(bottom)*.

Chapter 2

Fieldwork

A Personal Journey

$\mathcal{E}$thnographic fieldwork is a personal experience, not only because of the people with whom the researcher is interacting, but because it often forces the ethnographer to examine his or her own values and capabilities, and ability to adjust to a different culture. This is especially the case in this restudy because it forced me to reflect on myself as a researcher and as a person at different stages of my life: when I was a young and somewhat inexperienced ethnographer and now as an older ethnographer who has worked as part of a research team. I had to examine my research strengths and weaknesses, and my ability to adapt mentally and physically to the independence needed to conduct research as a lone ethnographer again rather than as a member of a research team. In this chapter, I examine ethnographic fieldwork as it pertains to my research activities with the Ga'dang in 1965–66 and 2010–11, beginning with a brief description of others who paved the way for my work.

Influential Predecessors

In preparing for my 1965–66 study, I drew inspiration from the long and storied history of anthropological fieldworkers who studied the hill cultures of Northern Luzon, several of whom may be considered the founders of modern American Anthropology. Some of these pioneers worked among the Ibaloi, Kankanay, Apayao, Ifugao, Kalinga, Tinguian, Ilongot, and other minority groups, all possessing a culture reminiscent of the Ga'dang. These fieldworkers worked in a time when logistics was a major daily challenge in the remote mountains of the Cordillera Central.

One of the earliest anthropologists to influence the direction of ethnology in the United States was Albert E. Jenks, who received his PhD in economics at the University of Wisconsin in 1899 and then turned his attention to ethnography when he went to the Philippines as a U.S. colonial officer (Soderstrom 2004). He created the ethnic categories for the 1903 Philippines census, was promoted to chief of the Ethnological Survey of the Philippines, oversaw the Philippines exhibit at the 1904 St. Louis World's Fair, and did research for his classic *The Bontoc Igorot* (1905), thus becoming the first American to publish a major anthropological study on the Philippines. In 1906, Jenks joined the University of Minnesota and later established the Department of Anthropology there.

Another prominent American researcher who worked with the highland people of Northern Luzon and contributed greatly to anthropology was Fay-Cooper Cole (Eggan 1963). Before going to the Philippines on a Field Museum of Chicago expedition, the ethnologist director of the museum, George A. Dorsey, sent Cole to Columbia University to study with Franz Boas for a semester and then to Germany for further training under Felix von Luschan. In the mountains of the Philippines, Cole started his research with the Tinguian, later presented as his PhD dissertation in 1914 at Columbia, and in 1915 his classic *Traditions of the Tinguian* was published. He worked as assistant curator of Malayan Ethnology at the Field Museum, and later retired as chair of the Department of Anthropology at the University of Chicago.

One of the most prolific and colorful students of the peoples of the mountains of Northern Luzon was Roy F. Barton (Kroeber 1949). While not trained in anthropology, he nonetheless contributed greatly to anthropology. The preeminent anthropologist A. L. Kroeber said of Barton, "Roy Franklin Barton produced some of the most gifted ethnography ever written in English, and especially on the Philippines people" (1949:91–95). Barton first went to the Philippines in 1906 as a civil service schoolteacher and then divided his time between the Philippines, Russia, and the U.S. until his death in 1947. Barton wrote several books on the hill peoples of the Philippines, the two most anthropologically important of which were *Ifugao Law* (1919) and *Philippines Pagans: The Autobiographies of Three Ifugaos* (1938). In a review of *Ifugao Law*, Laura Nader says, "It is a classic that we are now fortunate in having" (1970:15–27). People who knew Barton pointed out that he was an unusual man: a teacher, a student, a dentist, a researcher, a writer, and as Kroeber said, "Above all, he forgot himself over the objectives that rose in his view: his soul never rusted" (1949:94).

A brief discussion of the pioneers in Philippine ethnology would not be complete without acknowledging the contributions of H. Otley Beyer, the man most often considered the dean of Philippine anthropology (Zamora 1974). Although not well-known in the U.S., he was, nonetheless, a great influence on several generations of Filipino, American, and European anthropologists. One of my regrets in anthropology is that I did not get to know Professor Beyer until the last year of his life. He first went to the Philippines in 1905, left for further study in the U.S., returned to the Philippines in 1910, was a founding member of the University of the Philippines Department of

Anthropology, conducted pioneering research in prehistory and ethnology, counseled and befriended numerous local and foreign anthropologists, married an Ifugao woman, and was buried in an Ifugao burial shed in the mountains of Northern Luzon.

Beyer, with Barton and numerous other Americans, was interned in Japanese prison camps in the Philippines during World War II. It took Barton years to recover from the ordeal. Beyer was slightly more fortunate in that a Japanese man he had known during his brief study at Harvard served as a liaison between the Philippines and Japan during the Japanese occupation. Thus, much of Beyer's archaeological and ethnological collection, along with many of his manuscripts, were preserved while he was interned.

Soon after World War II, a new generation of anthropologists began conducting research in Northern Luzon and tutoring the next generation of researchers on the Philippines. For me and many of my generation, the intellectually most influential were Fred Eggan (1906–1991), Frank X. Lynch (1921–1978), Robert B. Fox (1918–1985), and Harold C. Conklin (1926–). Fred Eggan, best known for his research on social organization among Native Americans and as the person who led the synthesis between British and American social anthropology, also did extensive research with the hill peoples of Northern Luzon, and was the director of the University of Chicago Philippines Studies Program (Chicago 2009; Schusky and Eggan 1989). His research in the Northern Luzon community of Sagada remains a standard in social organization studies today (Eggan 1960).

During this period, Fr. Frank X. Lynch, S. J., a friend and mentor to many Philippine researchers, established the Institute of Philippine Culture at the Ateneo de Manila (Mangahas 2010; Yengoyan and Makil 1984). As a researcher concerned with the symbolism of meaning within Philippine society, Frank Lynch's most lasting contributions can be found in his leadership in the Philippine social sciences and the care he showed young scholars.

Robert Fox served the profession of anthropology as the Philippine presidential assistant for national minorities, and he served the Philippine people at the National Museum of the Philippines from 1948 to 1975 (Zamora 1986). While internationally known for his pioneering archaeological investigations in the Tabon Caves on Palawan, ethnographers were most influenced by his study of the Pinatubo Negrito (Fox 1953). This study was not only groundbreaking in the Philippines, but it predates many of the cognitive systems and human ecological oriented ethnographic studies of the 1960s. I am especially indebted to Robert Fox because he guided me in preparing my first major work on the mountain peoples of Luzon, which was published by the Philippine National Museum (Wallace 1969).

The most senior anthropologist associated with the Philippines today is Harold Conklin (Ng 2007). In 1944, Conklin arranged to be discharged from the U.S. Army in the Philippines where he immediately started his long, illustrious, and groundbreaking ethnographic and linguistic research career. In 1957, his classic ethnobotanical research was published as *Hanunóo Agricul-*

ture. Between 1961 and 1979, he conducted research among the Ifugao of Northern Luzon, producing in 1980 his *Ethnographic Atlas of Ifugao.* The distinguished Australian anthropologist William R. Geddes said of this work; "Without doubt the Atlas is the best survey of a tribal land-use ever produced" (1985:310).

Adapting to the Field and Maintaining Integrity

Most ethnographers adjust to the field setting with a little difficulty, but ultimately with success. I suspect the often-reported view of the inexperienced, ill-prepared, young novice wandering into an unknown situation and the accompanying culture shock reflect as much ethnographic drama as reality. Extremes in adjusting to the field setting may be illustrated with two cases, one a success and the other a failure, both involving anthropology and controversy.

It is clear that Napoleon Chagnon (1968), even with his acknowledged apprehension about working with the South American Yanomanö, adjusted successfully to a difficult cultural situation. By the standards of the social environment in which most ethnographers grow up, the Yanomanö were unpleasant groups of people during the 1960s. Regardless of the controversies surrounding the career of Chagnon, even his most severe critics must acknowledge his successful adjustment to Yanomanö life and the impact he had on students and the profession when he wrote in the introduction to his best-selling *Yanomanö: The Fierce People* (1968:5):

> I looked up and gasped when I saw a dozen burly, naked, filthy, hideous men staring at us down the shafts of their drawn arrows! Immense wads of green tobacco were stuck between their lower teeth and lips making them look even more hideous, and strands of dark-green slime dripped or hung from their noses.

It is a rarity, but not all ethnographers adjust well to the field setting. For example, especially germane to studies in the Philippines, William Jones, a PhD student of Franz Boas, worked successfully in North America with Native American Algonquin speakers. He adjusted so poorly to living with the Ilongot of the Philippines, however, that he certainly contributed to his own murder in 1909 (cf. Rideout 1912; R. Rosaldo 1980). When I first visited some Ilongot villages in 1965, located along the headwaters of the Cagayan River, I asked about William Jones, and numerous Ilongot were willing to discuss his death. According to them, in an argument with his Ilongot helpers over getting his collection of material goods downstream to the lowlands, Jones was killed by three Ilongot, one of whom he had lived with only a year earlier. What appeared to the locals as an excessive and disproportionate concern for his material goods may have been what got him killed.

Soon after reading William Jones' diary (1907–1909) at The Field Museum of Chicago in 1964, I commented to a distinguished mentor of mine something to the effect of, "No wonder they don't want this diary published. It is an embarrassment to anthropology. It's three-hundred pages on how to get killed." My statement reflected youthful idealism, so it should be noted that in Jones' defense, despite his Native American heritage and his PhD in anthropology, he was living in a time when the imperialistic interpretation of Kipling's "The White Man's Burden"—an interpretation that justified imperialism as a noble, but condescending, enterprise—was at its peak in the Philippines (R. Rosaldo 1980:8). It would appear that Jones embraced more than his share of the burden. It is unlikely that an ethnographer of today would make the same errors in cultural judgment that were made by Jones.

A less dramatic but more typical depiction of adapting to an ethnographic field situation than the examples of Chagnon and Jones is reported in Hortense Powdermaker's (1966) accounts of fieldwork in a Melanesian society; in a community in Mississippi; in Hollywood, California; and in an African mining township in Rhodesia (Zimbabwe Rhodesia). Each field experience presented a different challenge in adaptation for Powdermaker. She considered the field setting in the village of Lesu in New Guinea, in her words, "idyl" (1966:12). The people were friendly and outgoing, and she had few problems in adjusting. The situation in rural Mississippi was not nearly so comfortable for Powdermaker. She had to move very carefully between the lines set up by the white population and the African American population in the area, creating considerable field stress for her. Working in Hollywood also required some major adjustments. In her worlds, "The difficulties were very great; partly they were sociological and lay in the situation, and partly they were psychological and within me" (1966:13). Except for some methodological issues associated with quantification because the mining township population was 30,000, she had few problems adapting to the field setting in Zimbabwe Rhodesia. Her range of fieldwork experiences is probably representational of the experiences of most field ethnographers. Powdermaker succinctly and more accurately summarizes the adaptability of most ethnographers to the field setting in the title of her book: *Stranger and Friend* (1966).

The professional and personal emotions and ethics of adaption are also an important part of doing fieldwork. What can I do while maintaining my integrity, and what can I not do if I am to maintain my integrity (see Whiteford and Trotter 2008)? For example, I do not like to eat dog. But, if I do not eat dog in the rural Philippines while drinking with men, will my refusal erode my rapport? Part of my repulsion to eating dog is because of my Western background, part of it is because occasionally I like dogs better than some people, and finally, most dogs that are eaten in Asia, in my view, are cute puppies, making the situation for a Westerner even more difficult. Yet, I have eaten dog on many occasions. Is this a testament to my ability to adapt to the field setting or a statement on my lack of values? Maybe my ethics are situational. I believe eating dog, even though it offends me, shows my flexibility as an ethnographer. Importantly, however, an ethnographer must raise questions that reflect his or her personal and anthropological ethics: what if I am a vegetarian, what if I am a nondrinker of alcohol, and, while today only hypothetical, what would my response be if the meat were human?

A further issue closely related to how well the ethnographer adapts to the field setting is the degree to which he or she chooses to "go native." My experience suggests that how much an ethnographer should go native is determined by the local culture and politics, and the personality of the ethnographer. Among the Ga'dang, no matter how much I might try to go native, I can never be a Ga'dang, and more importantly, the culture is such that the Ga'dang do not want me to be a Ga'dang. I have a role as an outsider who is respected and accepted by the community and who blends in with the people of the community. They are pleased that I try to speak Ga'dang, I chew a little betel nut with them, and eat the local foods, but I am still an outsider. In 1965, my role was that of a student learning about the environment and Ga'dang culture. Now, my role is that of a senior researcher trying to learn how the environment and the Ga'dang have changed over a period of almost 50 years. In the past, I was living with a nonliterate population. Today, I am living with a literate population.

In the earlier study, I spoke Ga'dang, lived in a Ga'dang house, and lived very much like a Ga'dang. There were no other options. On occasion, I would join a social dance and chew betel nut as a rapport-building activity, but I was always an observer of ritual matters; I had no social responsibilities (except as an outsider), and I did not participate in any economic activity. I was "*kolak*," literally "brother" in Ga'dang, but also a term used to address "friend." In the restudy, the Ga'dang expected me to act like any other senior member of the community, which I did. I spoke Ga'dang as best I could after almost 50 years, and participated in community activities such as occasionally attending church services, hanging out where people shop for soft drinks and snacks, visiting households, and attending barangay functions. My view of carefully measuring the extent to which an ethnographer should go native was validated for me by the Ga'dang during the restudy when I was told about (and later met) a European man living in the northern Paracelis area who wears a G-string, chews betel nut daily, and has a Ga'dang family. For trying to be something he is not, the man is ridiculed by many Ga'dang, and his family is, to use a Ga'dang concept in translation, "to be pitied."

It has been argued that, "ethnographers have trouble with emotions . . . especially with how to write about them" (Beatty 2010:440). This is a skeptical view of ethnographic reporting that reflects too little faith in ethnographers, and our anthropological ancestors. If the ethnography gets in the way of the emotions, as Beatty suggests, the weakness may rest with ethnographers as writers, not as social scientists. It is not necessary to write in an uninspired and tedious manner just because we are writing in the social sciences. I try to convey to my students that except when dealing with detailed topics such as kinship and ecological model building, for example, if the reader has to study what is being written, the writer is doing a poor job of communicating. We can communicate effectively, and with the emotions of our subjects, and ourselves, without writing fiction. Some ethnographers have published novels, often under a pen name, but their novels are not their ethnographies nor are their ethnographies their novels. I have little difficulty in separating my ethnographic reporting from my fiction. Importantly, without narrating the personal interactions that are an integral feature of fieldwork, our ethnographies would be lifeless. This is not an argument for interpretive anthropology, but rather, it is a plea for honest and uncomplicated analysis and reporting.

It is the people in the ethnography, including the ethnographer, who give ethnographic studies a touch of humanity without distracting from the science of ethnographic research. For example, if the ethnographer is honest, he or she will admit a fondness for one person over another. In some cases, this is due to the knowledge the person possesses. In other cases, it may be just because the ethnographer "likes" the person. Just as over the years we all have had coworkers or acquaintances that we related to better than others, the same can be said for people in different cultures with whom I have interacted when gathering data. Admitting this is to accept that as individuals, people are different, regardless of their cultural background. This is no different than admitting that one person knows more about a specific cultural domain than another person. Most ethnographers probably have thought, for example, that a certain man is a very knowledgeable informant when it comes to providing cultural information on the food web, for example, but he is a very poor informant on birthing. Yet, the latter does not mean he is not a good informant.

If I write in my personal journal that I do not trust (regardless of the reason) a particular informant or that I spent the night throwing up my dinner, I know to study my field notes for that period with greater caution than usual; it is clear that the immediate physical and psychological condition of the ethnographer will condition his or her interpretation of the event of the time. As an ethnographer, I accept the inherent problems associated with reflexivity, but I do as much as possible to maintain my objectivity and to verify the information I gather in as many ways as necessary. Most ethnographic fieldworkers follow this approach. This acknowledges the subjectivity in the ethnographer's research, but it also acknowledges that steps are being taken to insure as much objectivity as possible. It is not necessarily a contradiction to recognize how reflexivity is a limiting factor in ethnographic research while at the same time adhering to the rigors of science.

Fieldwork: 1965–66 and Now

A student asked me whether doing fieldwork with the Ga'dang was more difficult in 1965 or 2010. My immediate response was that it was more difficult in 1965. As I thought about my answer, however, I realized that I should have been more guarded. In some aspects, fieldwork with the Ga'dang was more difficult in 1965, while in other aspects, it was more difficult in the restudy. A major issue during the original study was the time that had to be devoted to learning an unwritten language. While this was an invaluable cultural learning experience, it was nonetheless a time-consuming and sometimes frustrating activity. During the restudy, I could easily communicate in English, and in my inadequate Ilocano and Ga'dang.

Logistically, fieldwork with the Ga'dang was much more difficult in 1965–66 than in the restudy. In 1965, I had to walk for two days to a week from the nearest dirt road to reach the Ga'dang. This meant that I had to carry supplies, mainly rice and canned goods, to last three or more weeks, into the mountains because the Ga'dang could not afford to provide rice for me, although I could get vegetables and fruits from them. Even with a companion, carrying enough rice and other foods for several weeks into the mountains took considerable effort, especially since I had to cross two rivers (sometimes swollen and sometimes almost dry) before reaching the first Ga'dang village after leaving the lowlands. Carrying that much food in a backpack is a nuisance, and very tiring, to say the least. I tried using a small Asian pony, but that proved more trouble than any effort it might have saved. Swimming a swollen river with a pony is not only a comical sight but also a difficult experience. In the end, I finally settled on using a carabao sled. The supplies could be tied to the sled and, if necessary, transferred to a small boat when crossing a river. The carabao could swim alongside the boat.

In my restudy of the Ga'dang, I drove my old SUV directly to the villages. Any supplies I needed were easy to load and carry. The road was unpaved, steep, and rough, but even under rainy conditions, it took only two hours from the nearest lowland highway to reach the Ga'dang. By driving another hour, I could be in the Poblacion of Paracelis. The dirt road (except for a short cement stretch connected to a bridge over the Siffu River) from Bayongyong to the Poblacion generally followed a footpath that I originally walked in the 1965–66 study.

In 1965, my house, built on stilts, and typical for a small Ga'dang family, had a floor of split bamboo, which measured six by seven feet, and a small hearth in one corner. It was just large enough for me to stretch out while sleeping. The walls were made from woven bamboo, and it had a thatched roof. The hut was comfortable enough. Even during a typhoon, the thatched roof seldom leaked, although water often came through cracks in the walls. Its most uncomfortable feature was I could not stand upright in the interior of the house. My reading light was a beer bottle filled with kerosene and a rag. This was my Ga'dang home for almost two years.

Conversely, during the restudy, I had a hotel room in a town two hours' driving distance, and I also had a room with an elderly Ga'dang man and woman whose house was constructed from planked boards; it had a galvanized roof and consisted of four rooms. There was electricity, and I could easily stand up in the rooms.

I spent far less time during the restudy on personal matters (cooking, bathing, washing clothes, etc.) than I did in 1965. During the earlier study, I did my own cooking, and bathing and washing clothes was done in a moun-

Traveling to the mountains, 1965 *(top)*.
Traveling to the lowlands, 2010 *(bottom)*.

tain stream located down an almost 80-degree embankment. Drinking water was a constant concern. In the restudy, water was piped into the village from a mountain spring (for all but three or so months a year), so bathing was a simple task. During the dry season or when the water hoses broke, water came from the nearby river. I ate with a family. If I decided to spend some time in the closest town, I ate in local restaurants, and spent the nights in a small hotel. When in town, the greatest demand on my time was the two hours it took for me to drive to the village.

Because I had electricity during the restudy, recording field notes on a laptop computer was far more efficient than typing them on a portable typewriter. With search, find, backup, and other features, it was much easier to store and analyze data. A minor and somewhat frustrating problem I encountered in using my field notes from 1965–66 was, after almost two years with the Ga'dang, I had started writing many of my notes in Ga'dang rather than in English. In retrospect, I should have always translated what I had written. At the time, I was not anticipating the future.

Although in 2010–11 there are no cell towers in the immediate vicinity of the Ga'dang community of Bananao, it was possible to get a cell signal in certain locations. Even though I could not receive calls unless I went to one of these locations, communicating with the outside world was a relatively easy matter. The cell signal, however, was too weak and sporadic to use a cell service to access the Internet. Conversely, in 1965, there was no efficient way to communicate with the outside world except by walking a day or more, riding a jeepney for several hours, and then taking a bus to a major city. All this activity was necessary just to send a telegraph. Telephones simply were not available in the Cagayan Valley. For example, I once was on the Ga'dang side of the Magat River when a typhoon entered the area. There was no way to know the typhoon was approaching because there were no radios in my Ga'dang village. I had been in the mountains for a month, and people in a small Ilocano community in the Cagayan Valley were expecting me to return any day. I simply had to trust that the people expecting me would figure out that the typhoon had me trapped and I would be back as soon as possible. If I had been stranded by a typhoon in 2010–11, I easily would have walked up a hill to an active signal point, made a cell call, and informed them of my situation.

Finding Ga'dang settlements was no easy matter in 1965, not because the Ga'dang tried to hide them, but because of my naiveté. When I arrived in the Philippines, I rented a small house in the province of Isabela, which was located a few kilometers east of the Magat River because I was told that there were some Ga'dang villages west of the Magat along the Cordillera Central. The small house I found to rent was in a typical rural Philippine village. It had a population of around a thousand people, a rural market, a dirt road, and no electricity. From there, I started my hunt for Ga'dang settlements.

Once settled in Isabela, I needed to locate someone who spoke Ga'dang, Ilocano, and English to serve as my translator. I had heard of a young Filipino about my age who was a Cagayano Christian Gaddang, lived in an Ilocano community, and I was told that he spoke English. His village was only about four hours walking from where I was located, so I went to see him. Unfortunately, when I arrived in his village, I was told that he was in jail in a nearby town—suspected of murder. All of his neighbors, however, defended him; they argued that he was not guilty and even offered suggestions for identifying another man as the murderer. After I spent a week discussing the situation with the local police, and with a small incentive, the young man was released from jail. He agreed to work for me as my interpreter. Within a year, another man was convicted of the murder.

My initial search for the Ga'dang proved more difficult than I expected. The lowland people with whom I asked about the Ga'dang kept telling me they had never heard of the Ga'dang. They did say, however, that there were Kalinga who occasionally came into town to sell their bamboo and to shop in the market. In time, I learned that "kalinga" was a term used in common Cagayan Valley Ilocano meaning "wild men of the forest." At the time, I thought the lowlanders were referring to the ethnic group called Kalinga. I had no idea that "kalinga" was a general gloss used in the Cagayan Valley for so-called dangerous hill peoples.

My first encounter with a Ga'dang was eventful—at least it made me uncomfortable and gave me cause to wonder what I was doing in the mountains of the Philippines, especially considering the many times I had been warned not to go. It was a hot day, and I was resting on a rotting felled tree. My Ga'dang-speaking companion had excused himself to take care of some physical needs, when I looked along the path from which I had just walked and saw three men, each dressed in a G-string (*abag*), each with large machete (*bolo* or *palatao*) strapped to his waist, and each with red betel nut juices seeping from his lips. The man leading the group seemed to be blind in one eye, was carrying a spear, and had a head axe tucked in his abag. He was a frightening sight to me; all three appeared threatening. We looked at one another, neither of us knowing what to say. To my good fortune, my companion appeared and I was able to have a cautious conversation with the Ga'dang man leading the group.

The most telling thing about my first encounter with the Ga'dang did not become apparent for several months. After I had learned some Ga'dang and had become friends with the Ga'dang man who had only one good eye, late one cool night I was sitting with him and three other Ga'dang near the hearth drinking cheap gin. During the evening, he looked at me and said, "Kolak . . . the first time I saw you, I was very frightened. I was scared of you." When I told him I had a similar reaction to him, we both had a good laugh.

Establishing rapport with the Ga'dang in 1965 was not easy. Initially, the Ga'dang were uncomfortable with me living in the village, or at least they did not know what to do with me, so they allowed me to stay in an abandoned hut out of sight of the village. I felt very isolated. I knew I was missing information by not being able to see what was happening in the village. In time, however, with patience and with the development of trust, I was allowed to build a small house within the village, and soon was interacting daily with all members of the settlement.

Establishing rapport in Bayongyong during the restudy was accomplished with little difficulty. Because I had visited friends in the community over a period of many years, I was known by some of the Ga'dang. Even though my closest friends were dead by the time of the restudy, I had a legitimate place in the community as an accepted outsider. I was to the older generation "kolak," technically meaning "brother," but as noted, a term also used to denote "friend." A significant rapport-building feature of my reintroduction to the Ga'dang was photocopies of photographs from the 1965–66 study—pictures of me with children who are now adults and pictures of the parents and grandparents of current residents of the community. These photographs fascinated both old and young people, the former because it reminded them of the past, and the latter because it showed them what life was like for their grandparents and parents.

Life in a Ga'dang village 45 years ago was markedly different from life in a Ga'dang village today. Two examples, one from 1966 and the other from 2010, both taken directly from my field notes (including shorthand and questionable grammar) will serve to illustrate. These two examples are not necessarily typical, nor are they atypical. They are examples of two days reflecting mainly the Ga'dang of a different time and a different place.

To set the stage, and convey the Ga'dang in a more humanistic manner, a brief description of the people involved is worthwhile. In the example from the earlier study, Laya was a small Ga'dang settlement located in a forest, a day's walk from Pakak. Laya was abandoned in the early 1970s and some of the residents moved to Bayongyong. Many of the men wore the abag, and several of the women were often shirtless. This was their daily attire when working. On this day in 1966, however, many were dressed in their finest skirts, beads, betel bags, and jackets because they were attending a two-day ritual (*makadwa*) held in support of a long and productive life of a Ga'dang couple and for the couple to demonstrate that they were sufficiently wealthy to fund the ceremony. The primary actor in this event was Tabuong, a female medium, about 65 years of age, and renowned throughout the Ga'dang area for her skills as a medium, and for going into a trance. She was assisted by Duwayen, a male medium, about 70 years of age, from Pakak and known for his knowledge of ritual chanting. All activities were carried out in Ga'dang.

In the example from the restudy, a few Ga'dang and I left Bayongyong in my old SUV for the Poblacion of Paracelis. All my passengers were dressed in Western cloths, including shoes or flip-flops. My passengers were Josie, a 29-year-old woman who was the daughter of one of my dearest Ga'dang friends (who died three years ago); Sollay, a 75-year-old man who converted to Christianity when he was in his 50s; Aning, a 55-year-old woman I had known when she was a ten-year-old child; and Adang, a 40-year-old woman I did not know well, but who needed a ride to Paracelis. Our conversations were conducted in a mixture of Ga'dang, Ilocano, and English.

Fields notes, June 6, 1966, Laya

07:00   I have been up since 05:00. I had breakfast of rice and a boiled egg. The makamba has started again. Tabuong is the *makamong* [female medium] and Duwayen is the *mabayen* [male medium]. They are chanting again. The woman in the house next door is pounding rice for the events this afternoon. The man and woman of the house where the makadwa is being held are required to do no work. The makadwa is being held for them. Tabuong was given new beads last night to wear this morning.

07:30   Tabuong and Duwayen have stopped chanting and have gone to the house across the path to eat breakfast. They did not stop chanting until around midnight last night so I am sure they are very tired. They started chanting early this morning.

09:00   There has been absolutely no ritual activity going on for the past hour and one-half. People are just sitting around talking. Some are napping.

10:00   People are beginning to arrive from different Ga'dang communities. Nothing, however, appears to be going on . . . people are just visiting. I do notice that large quantities of rice have been brought into the house. Maybe at least a cavan [approximately 2.13 U.S. bushels or 50 kg].

11:00   During the past hour, I have been working with Duwayen trying to transcribe his mabayen songs. These songs, for the most part, are stories about the Ga'dang, and sung in a slow, one octave and 4/4 time cadence. The average Ga'dang does not understand the songs as they are sung in a special mabayen language (a form of archaic Ga'dang). The song or story I have been working on with Duwayen is entitled *kokan-weno alotu* or "The Saying of Alotu." It will take me hours when I return to Pakak to finish transcribing and understanding this song.

11:15   The sacrificial pig has been carried to the house. Tabuong has placed a stick and water in the ear of the pig and, from reading the squeals it makes, told us that it has passed all the tests and it is ready to be killed. Duwayen kills the pig by sticking a thin sharp knife into its throat that cuts through the jugular vein. As it starts to bleed out, some of the blood is placed in a banana leaf. Tabuong takes some of the blood from the leaf and spots her head and the faces of the woman and the man of the house. This is to aid in insuring a long life.

11:30   Duwayen has about finished overseeing the butchering of the pig.

12:00   They have finished butchering the pig. Most of us have been sitting around talking and resting. The neighbors, men and woman, are chopping the pig into pieces for cooking, the women are pounding rice and preparing to cook it.

14:30   The pig is cooking. Tabuong and Duwayen each receive a shoulder and a hip, and they split the head, as payment for the ceremonial work they have been doing the past two days. As was done yesterday, the pig was cooked in pots at the house of the sponsoring couple.

16:00   We have not eaten yet. Most of us took a short nap while the pig and rice were being cooked. Both Duwayen and Tabuong started singing about 30 minutes ago. Tabuong stopped for a while to take a little rice and meat, wrap it in a banana leaf, and offer it to the *anitu* [spiritual power]. Duwayen continues singing the "The Saying of Alotu" or some song much like that one.

17:30   We have finally eaten. The meal was standard ceremonial food: rice and boiled pork. Duwayen and Tabuong have stopped singing for now. Everybody is happy because we had a good meal. The children were fed first, followed by the adults. I was not treated any differently than any other Ga'dang. I hear the gongs starting to play outside.

18:00   People are starting to arrive from other villages. Some of the people of Laya are putting on different clothes and getting ready for the social dancing of the evening.

19:30   There are now many people surrounding the house. I think there must be at least 35 people here. Tabuong and Duwayen continue singing. No one is paying any attention to them. People are much more interested in the social dancing . . . the gongs are very loud and the dancing by both men and women seems very animated and excited. The men and women are all dressed in their finest abag and skirts, and obviously showing off their dancing skills. There is a lot of drinking going on by the men . . . mainly cheap commercially made gin.

20:30   Tabuong starts dancing. She is joined by her assistant makamong, a some-what younger woman. The social dancers move away to watch Tabuong and her assistant. The gong players start to play faster and louder. . . . Tabuong moves away from the younger woman. The assistant makamong is now dancing alone. As the gong sounds get louder and even faster, there are screams from the dancer, and she is bouncing higher and higher. Just like Tabuong did last night, it seems to me that the assistant's eyes are starting to see nothing. She is starting to shake wildly. Her body jerks. She could fall so Tabuong stands near her. Two men stand beside her. Suddenly, she collapses and the men catch her. She is carried into the house to rest.

21:00   The social dancing started not long after the assistant makamong fainted. I am told that, just as Tabuong did last night, the assistant became possessed by anitu, or she became *na'unagon* . . . *anitu*—"anitu gets inside the body."

22:30   Around 22:00 a strong wind and a heavy rain came up so we all fled into nearby houses. It was crowded, hot, and many of the men were drinking to the point that some of them were getting drunk and generally becoming unruly. A young drunk got into several verbal skirmishes with some of the men from Pakak. The young man pushed Duwayen off the porch. Duwayen retaliated by taking his bolo and struck the young man on the head with the flat side of the bolo. The young man fell to the ground. I decided it was time for me to leave. I retreated to an abandoned tree house at the edge of the village, climbed up the ladder, pulled the ladder up behind me . . . and here I plan to stay and sleep.

Field notes, June 12, 2010, Bayongyong, Paracelis Poblacion

09:00   I picked up Josie and her daughter, age two, at the river and we are getting ready to go to Paracelis. Sollay is going with us. Aning and Adang also are going with us. Around 20 other Ga'dang have already left for Paracelis in a truck. It should be an interesting day in Paracelis . . . it is Philippine Independence Day. It has been raining, but since I have a four-wheel-drive vehicle, we should not have any problems. Josie is going to take her daughter to see the doctor because the child has been having an elevated temperature for the past four days. The rest of us will either participate in the celebrations or watch the celebrations.

10:15 We have arrived in the Poblacion of Paracelis after an uneventful ride. We stopped along the road and picked up two more Ga'dang needing a ride to Paracelis. While driving, I was able to ask many questions about the differences between uma cultivation and plow farming.

11:00 Paracelis is very crowded today. I had to park beyond the market area. It is Independence Day and there is not only an all-day program going on in front of the municipal building, but there is a market and a traveling carnival in town. The parade has just started.

12:00 The parade is a big event. Most high schools and villages in the Munici-pality of Paracelis with a marching band are participating. Some of the groups in the parade are senior citizens. Sollay and his group of 18 senior citizens are wearing blue vests embroidered with "Senior Citizens of Bananao" on the back in yellow. This is a patriotic event, with the parade being led by the local police force carrying a Philippine flag. Marching bands, majorettes, and glockenspiel players dressed in their finest and most colorful costumes are marching and strutting to the sounds of John

Independence Day parade in Paracelis, 2010.

Phillip Sousa. Two *bakla*, in full transvestite dress (majorette costumes), a sight that would not have been seen among the Ga'dang 50 years ago, are prancing and strutting in front of one of the bands.

13:30 Just had lunch with the owner of a small market food shop. Upland rice and boiled chicken. Pretty tasty. The owner of the shop is a Balangao speaker from Natonin. According to him, he moved to Paracelis 20 years ago when he married his Ga'dang wife. He tells me that there are many marriages between Balangao and Ga'dang speakers because the two groups have a long history together. Despite their long history of intermarriage, there have been conflicts between the Ga'dang and the Balangao. The Balangao have pushed down the Cordillera, grabbing land from the Ga'dang, while the Ilocano have pushed up from the Cagayan Valley, taking land from the Ga'dang.

14:00 Josie just found me eating lunch. She has taken her daughter to a private physician and he has sent her to the local provincial hospital to have some tests run on her daughter. It is only about 200 meters from here so I will walk with her to the hospital.

14:30 I'm waiting for Josie in front of the Paracelis District Hospital. According to Josie, she has papers from the private physician, which will allow the hospital to take blood and urine from her daughter. The hospital is understaffed and has 25 beds. It is constructed from cement blocks, has a galvanized roof, and is considered the new hospital because the old hospital was rendered unusable after a 2006 landslide. By Western standards, it is wholly inadequate, grimy, in need of cleaning and paint, but by rural Philippines standards, it seems typical to me.

15:00 It seems Josie will be a while so I am going up to the municipal building . . . the Paracelis Municipal Hall . . . to watch the program.

15:30 On the way to the hall I stop and watch numerous people participate in gambling games, especially those type of games where you bounce a ping pong ball and try to land in a certain hole or roll a colored die in hope of it stopping on the right color. The stop costs me a hundred pesos.

16:00 There must be 300 people in front of the Municipal Hall watching some sort of game or race going on. It is a total mystery to me what they are doing. Elderly women—six teams of six women—a few of them dressed in native skirts over Westerns skirts, are removing items of clothing, placing them on the ground to form a long string of items of clothing as competition to arrive at the other side of the field in front of the Municipal Hall.

16:30 The winning team of women are from Butigue. The last woman won for her team by placing her hat down to complete the line of clothing just over the finish line. I will ask someone later what I have just witnessed. Everybody seems to be having great fun.

17:00 While watching the games, I meet the local DENR representative. He is in charge of working with farm families in the Municipality of Paracelis to try and determine the many conflicting claims for land in the area by Ga'dang, Balangao, Ilocano, Ifugao, and others. According to him, some of the conflicting land claims may never be resolved. He is married to the local municipal agricultural officer. I need to get to know them both much better.

17:30 Josie and Sollay just joined me. The blood and urine tests on Josie's little girl show nothing. The physician prescribed some antibiotics for the child. Josie tells me she will take her daughter to a local healer in Bayongyong tomorrow if the fever is still present.

18:00 My vehicle is full. It's good that it has a third seat in the back. Beside Josie and Sollay, and Aning and Adang, four more Ga'dang are riding back with us.

19:30 The trip back to Bayongyong and the house of Sollay is uneventful. I keep thinking that the daily events could have taken place almost anywhere in the rural Philippines. Except for a few elderly women who had on the colorful skirts of the Ga'dang and some beads, I saw no traditional clothing being worn. I did not see one abag. For me, there seems to be nothing in particular that could be called "Ga'dang" about the events of the day. I have a can of corned beef so that will be my contribution to dinner tonight. Corned beef, upland rice, and a banana or two will make a fine dinner.

While the logistics of doing fieldwork with the Ga'dang were more demanding in the 1960s, certain features of fieldwork during the restudy were more challenging. Most of these challenges have to do with my personality and the way I perceive the Ga'dang, and the way the Ga'dang perceive me.

One of the more difficult aspects of interacting with the Ga'dang in the restudy was adjusting to my status as an accepted but elderly outsider. Since I had been friends with some people's fathers and mothers, the Ga'dang of Bayongyong tended to treat me as an elderly person, who by Ga'dang standards already should be dead. Most of my old Ga'dang friends were dead. Consequently, I was often afforded a status that would have been due my Ga'dang peers if they were still alive. Concurrently, I had some difficulty adjusting to being treated as an old person—afu (term for grandparent or respected elder) rather than kolak. Occasionally, I was frustrated by being treated as though I could not walk up a particular mountain, for example, when I knew I could walk up the mountain with little difficulty. In the earlier study, I was a young man and the Ga'dang assumption was that I could walk far, swim the river, or climb the mountain just as they could. In addition, as a young man during the original study, I was able to attach myself to older men and women as a student who wanted to learn the language and culture. There are certain advantages when doing fieldwork to be able to pretend naiveté.

Another factor that required considerable adjustment on my part during the restudy was accepting that I knew more about Ga'dang traditional culture than most of the Ga'dang. As noted, many of the Ga'dang with whom I had interacted on a daily basis, and whom I trusted to provide thoughtful answers to my questions, were dead. One man and one woman of my age living in Bayongyong have had strokes, and because they were unable to receive the

An elderly woman in author's 1965 study.

Respected elder in Bayongyong, 2010.

proper brain therapy, they never fully recovered. Both lost much of their ability to communicate. One of my old friends converted to Christianity, and according to him, "the past is the past." He does not want to think of the Ga'dang of the past. For him, the Ga'dang culture of the past was what he called "uncivilized." As will be shown later, many of the younger people simply did not know a great deal about their cultural heritage.

Often, when I asked a younger Ga'dang a question about some form of culturally based behavior, and the answer was very different from what I expected, I was tempted to tell the person what the practice was 45 years ago. Occasionally I would use a Ga'dang term, which was meaningless to the person with whom I was talking. Then, I would have to figure out a way to ask the question in another way to make sure I was not mispronouncing the Ga'dang term. Sometimes, what was to me the most simple of Ga'dang concepts—such as a slash-and-burn or uma cultivation technique—would prompt a response, which I knew to be far from what it would have been years ago. I had to keep reminding myself that I was not the informant.

As a final observation of fieldwork then and now, I had to adjust my expectations to fit the times. During the 1965–66 study, I expected to learn something new almost every time I asked a question, every time I went to a new village, or every time I witnessed a ritual. During the restudy, it seems that everything I saw I had seen before and every question I asked had an answer I had heard before. Perhaps this was due to cynicism and age. Perhaps it was due to familiarity and the many years I have spent living in the rural Philippines. Whatever the reasons, the Ga'dang of today are certainly not as culturally striking or unique as they were in 1965. The days of the abag, the colorful skirt woven on a back strap loom, the gold earrings, the spears, and elaborate ceremonies with all-night social dancing are gone. Research during the earlier study was tedious, but it was a relatively straightforward activity to view, ask about, and record strikingly different cultural things and activities. Examining the obvious and the common in the restudy required me to rethink the sociology of cultural behavior. I had to find the excitement that goes with discovery in the changes that accompany modernization.

Chapter 3

Trading a G-String for a Pair of Pants

Material Change

$\mathcal{I}$n a time not too long ago, in almost any place in Asia, an ethnographer could identify a cultural group by observing the construction of the houses, the design and color of the clothing, or the shape of the local headgear. This is no longer the case. Previously distinct cultures are blending, especially in the domain of material culture, such that under the umbrella of modernization, they are becoming visually difficult to identify. Northern Luzon is no exception to this pattern.

As noted earlier, two of the major homogenizers of material culture throughout Southeast Asia have been the T-shirt and the so-called gimme cap. Clearly, the inexpensive advertising afforded local and national politicians and corporations by printing their logo on T-shirts or caps has proved to be a very effective way of promoting themselves or their products. It also provides clothing for poor people, and it is a social equalizer. In the rural Philippines, this form of advertising was popularized by politicians during the 1970s, it was refined by businesses in the 1980s, and it is now a practice of NGOs, banks, and small and large businesses. On almost any day in Bay-ongyong, T-shirts and gimme caps with advertisements on them can be seen.

In this chapter, I examine the material culture of the Ga'dang in the past and the present and show how the changes have influenced Ga'dang life.

Dressing Ga'dang

Most of the Ga'dang in the 1965 study either dressed in traditional Ga'dang attire or mixed Western clothes with traditional items of dress. Only a few men dressed Western on a regular basis. Daily dress was different from the clothes a man would wear if he were attending a social and/or ceremonial function. In the village, during a normal day, a man would wear a simple abag, woven on a back-strap loom by his wife or another woman relative. The only decoration on the abag was in the pattern of the weaving. In 1965, some of the weavers still used dyes created from local materials, although some commercial dyes were beginning to enter the community. If the man, for example, was planning to work in the fields or visit someone in another village, he might wear a sleeveless T-shirt and either a straw hat or bandana on his head. If the man was older, he might wear a Western-style sport jacket, often saved from World War II, with his abag. Almost all men would have a machete (palatao)

Ga'dang in the village of Cabanuangan, 1965.

strapped around their waist held by a woven rattan belt. For the most part, each man also would have a betel bag (*sayay*), a red cloth bag housing betel nut, mollusk shells to pound into lime powder, and maybe some tobacco or betel leaves, hanging around this neck. He might have in his bag a bamboo container with a carved animal bone stopper in which to pound his shells into lime powder. Shoes or slippers were seldom used by the Ga'dang in the 1960s.

Many men had short, Western-style haircuts, while other men wore their hair shoulder length with straight bangs. When asked why they cut their hair in a Western style, the common response was because they could go into the lowland villages and be less likely to be singled out as hill people. Often when I would be walking to the lowlands with a group of Ga'dang men, we would stop before we arrived near a town, and the men would slip on a pair of long trousers to cover their abag, somehow believing they would not be recognized as mountain people, or at least they would blend in better with the lowlanders.

Men's clothing for ceremonial and social dancing was much more elaborate and colorful than clothing for daily wear. A man's dress abag was ladened with small glass beads, often dominated by the color white with orange or red horizontal stripes. Sometimes the abag had beaded fringe. In addition, he would wear a short jacket, woven in blue, red, and orange with beads.

A man's ceremonial dress, 1966.

Larger beads, some commercial and some antique European or Chinese glass beads, would be worn around his neck, although not nearly as many as a woman might wear. He also might wear brass arm bracelets. As a final touch, he would have on a cape, woven on a back-strap loom, dark blue and red in color, hanging down to his ankles. Sometimes he might wear a headpiece made from bird feathers. When dressed in this elaborate attire, he seldom wore a machete.

Ordinary daily wear for women consisted of nothing more than a skirt, beads, and earrings. Even in the 1960s, as many women wore skirts made from Western-made fabrics as those who wore skirts woven on a back-strap loom. Around the village, the women more often than not went bare breasted. If they traveled to another village or town, they wore a Western style blouse over a Western skirt or a traditional woven skirt. The traditional skirt, like the everyday abag, was decorated by the colors in the weaving, usually dark blue and dull red. Most all women wore their necklaces of colorful beads daily, often heirloom beads they inherited from their mothers. Women seldom were without their beaded earrings.

During cultural celebrations and/or social dances, Ga'dang women dressed in their finest clothing. A woven wraparound skirt in dark blue and red, with heavily beaded horizontal stripes in white, was the standard. Women also wore a jacket, usually long sleeved, in red or blue with a small beaded decoration on the sleeves. Over her shoulders, she might wear a red scarf with a beaded decoration at the four corners. A woven sash in matching colors could be wrapped around her waist. Sometimes a woman would wear a beaded skullcap. During celebrations, women always wore their finest beads, sometimes as many as five or six strings fitted snugly around the neck, and another six to eight might hang down to the waist. Earrings were necessary for ceremonies.

In the 1960s, most middle-aged and older women and men had tattoos, especially on their arms, hands, and fingers, although the practice was disappearing among younger people. The same also applied to the practice of women and men filing their teeth. For the traditional Ga'dang, filing the canine teeth flat to the level of the incisors created a pleasant contrast with a person's red lips when chewing betel.

Today, the dress of most Ga'dang men and women is indistinguishable from any other rural Filipino. On an everyday basis, the men wear long pants, jeans if they can afford them, and rubber flip-flops. Inside the house, going without footwear is the norm for both men and women. The women wear skirts, blouses, and long and short pants for everyday dress. If going to the fields to work, men and women usually wear a straw hat or a gimme cap. Some Ga'dang women still wear a few strings of colorful beads. If some of the beads are antique, they are usually quick to note it as most of the beads now are plastic copies of old beads, usually purchased from a traveling Kalinga saleswoman.

Ga'dang in the village of Bayongyong, 2010.

Traditional attire—skirts, G-strings, betel nut bags, capes, and jackets—are seldom seen among the Ga'dang today. An elderly Ga'dang friend of mine who in the past wore an abag daily said to me one afternoon, "I sometimes wear my string in the house at night. Never outside! I don't want people to think I'm uncivilized." When worn, traditional attire is for events emphasizing Ga'dang or mountain cultural pride such as the annual Founders Day fiesta. When the men, usually young, wear an abag to dance at such a fiesta, they more often than not wear Western undershorts under the string. Weaving on a back-strap loom is a lost art except for a couple women living in the Poblacion who weave for the tourist trade.

When going to town, attending a local or national celebration, a funeral, a wedding, or church, Ga'dang men and women currently dress in their finest clothing—all Western in style. The quality and quantity of a family's clothing is determined by its economic status. Men who can afford it sometimes wear sneakers. Women wear the latest-fashion flats they can afford.

Traditionally, young Ga'dang children often wore only an old, hand-me-down T-shirt. The same applies to contemporary Ga'dang young children. By the time a child was around ten, girls would wear a dress or skirt, and boys would wear pants or a G-string. By the age of 12, the girls were considered young women and the boys were young men, so they dressed appropriately, but by the time of the earlier study, the traditional skirts and abag were disappearing for the young people. Today, school-age children dress in Western attire. As teenagers, they want, and if the family can afford it, the latest fashion clothes.

Most Ga'dang over the age of 30 continue to chew betel nut. Rather than carrying their betel nut paraphernalia in a fancy neck bag, men tend to keep betel materials in their pocket and women tend to carry a small bag made of old cloth or a small purse. Sometimes a man or woman will wear a fanny-pack to carry the betel nut paraphernalia. The container in which the shell is pounded into lime powder is no longer bamboo with an animal bone stopper; now it commonly may be a small bottle.

Traditionally, beads were an integral feature of Ga'dang culture. During the 1965–66 study, ancient Chinese, Indian, and European beads of glass, porcelain, quartz, brass, silver, and even gold were combined to make necklaces, earrings, and decoration on clothing. Beads were also used in numerous cultural events, such as betrothal, spouse exchange, rites of passage, and curing rituals; to pay debts; and as payments for committing a cultural wrong. Many of the beads had a specific value placed on them. For example, a gold bead in a special earring used in securing a wife could have a value of up to three water buffalo. Other types of beads might have a value of a pig or two. Common beads—used as fillers between the high-value beads and purchased from lowland traders—had little value. There were many different types of beads, all with specific name designations. Beads in the form of necklaces, earrings, and bracelets were passed from generation to generation, occasionally from father to son, but more often from mother to daughter. During the 1965–66 study, there was an elaborate lexical taxonomy associated with Ga'dang beads. For example, if the researcher asked a Ga'dang man or woman about beads, he or she would reply with a question related to what kind of beads—*lufay, kiring, bukat, gatok*? In short, there were seven major categories of Ga'dang beads in my original study, many of which could be ordered into subcategories of beads.

Today, the necklaces, and traditional earrings and bracelets, are generally only worn by women over 40 years of age, and even then, the number of women wearing traditional bead jewelry is uncommon. Most adults, however, perceive beads as being a part of Ga'dang culture, although not many antique beads remain with the Ga'dang. When asked about the absence of beads and other forms of jewelry, the common answer from women was "we sold them." The antique dealers from Manila and Baguio often travel to the remote areas of the Philippines in search of traditional tribal jewelry, clothing, weapons, carvings, and Chinese antique pottery. Since the Ga'dang were one of the groups in the mountains that tended to maintain their traditional culture longer than some other ethnic groups, the demand for their ethnically based material goods has been great. The antique dealers pay a relatively small price for the ethnic items, although it may seem like a good price to the Ga'dang seller. The dealers then sell the ethnic items to tourists in the cities or on the Internet for a very handsome profit. It is a form of "culture for sale," similar to standing along the side of the highway in native dress and charging tourists to take a photograph, common in other parts of Mountain Province.

Around the House

In the 1965–66 study, Ga'dang families moved on average every 6.2 years to a new location, mainly following the forests for uma cultivation. Traditional houses were small and had only one room, even if the family had four or five children. On rare occasion, the house might have two rooms. Typically, the floor space would be eight by ten feet, maybe as large as ten by ten feet. A Ga'dang house was constructed three to five feet above the ground on support posts made from small trees. Sometimes, these support posts were trees that were only trimmed, not cut down. The walls of the house were made from flattened bamboo strips woven together, or they were upright bamboo. The roof consisted of cogon thatching, and the floor was made from split bamboo. The bamboo, thatching, and support structure were tied together by split rattan, although metal wire as a tying material was beginning to enter the Ga'dang community by 1965. Nails were still not used. People entered the house by climbing up a bamboo ladder.

All Ga'dang houses were very much the same inside. In one corner of the house was a flat hearth, usually to the left as a person entered the house, but not always. Above the hearth, metal plates covered in blue and white baked enamel, and often chipped, were stored along with cooking utensils. These were usually stuck in between the thatching and the ceiling supports. In the corner at the other end of the house was usually some sort of storage unit like a trunk where clothing and any items of value might be stored.

Hanging from the ceiling of the house, each in a culturally defined place, were six house *unting*—items of supernatural importance, which protected the family from catastrophic events and evil spirits. All of these house unting were important, but the most important, around which the others revolved, was a bundle of family clothing (e.g., abag, skirt, etc.) that had been passed down from generation to generation. In the view of the Ga'dang, without the house unting, the house was not Ga'dang. (Unting is discussed in more detail in chapter 6.) Eating, sleeping, and lounging were done on the floor in Ga'dang houses. Chairs, stools, and beds were not a part of the house furnishings.

Traditionally, the Ga'dang were known for their houses built in trees. While not common in the 1960s, some of these houses still existed. The tree houses were like any other Ga'dang house except that they were built anywhere from 12 to 20 feet above the ground, usually using more than one tree as support. According to Ga'dang, the reason for building the house so high off the ground was for safety. After the ladder was pulled up at night, it would have been extremely difficult for anyone to attack the people sleeping in the house. I could find no examples of tree houses in the Ga'dang area today.

The author's house, 1965 *(top)*.
A modest Ga'dang house in Bayongyong, 2011 *(bottom)*.

A 100 percent survey of the 22 households in Bayongyong shows clear changes in the use of Ga'dang household material since 1965. My visual survey of the rest of Bananao suggests that Bayongyong is representative of this area.

There is nothing unique about Ga'dang houses in Bayongyong and the greater Paracelis area today. The families no longer find it necessary to follow the forests because the people are now permanent field farmers. The Ga'dang of the Paracelis area are settled in permanent villages. The houses are constructed and look very much like any other rural Filipino house, except for a very few houses, belonging to very poor and/or very old families, that are still small and traditional in orientation. The days of the house with flattened and woven bamboo walls are gone. Today, the house may be built on the ground or on two- or three-foot support pilings, but is constructed from upright bamboo, sawed plank boards, or cement blocks. For example, 50 percent of the houses in Bayongyong are constructed from cement blocks and the other 50 percent are constructed from wood or upright bamboo, or a combination of wood, bamboo, and cement blocks. Almost all roofs are made from galvanized steel, although a few thatched roofs still exist especially among poorer families. In Bayongyong, 90 percent of the houses have galvanized roofs, with only two houses having cogon thatching as a roof. In Bayongyong, 50 percent of the houses have a cement floor, and the other 50 percent of the houses have a dirt floor.

Typically, modern Ga'dang houses have two to three rooms. Often the house has an attached kitchen as a room, and one or two other rooms. Frequently, the kitchen is at floor level, next to a floor-level sitting and eating area, situated next to one or two sleeping rooms built on pilings such that to enter the sleeping area a person has to climb a short ladder. The kitchen area is generally small, maybe six feet wide and 12 feet long. The sitting area might be 12 feet by eight feet. The elevated sleeping area can be as wide as 12 feet and as long as 15 feet, and divided into two rooms. In Bayongyong, two houses have only one room. The house with the largest number of rooms has five. The houses in Bayongyong average 2.1 rooms.

I could identify only four houses in the barangay of Bananao that had even a few items of the house unting hanging inside the house. In two cases, a very small bamboo house had been constructed near the main house especially to hold the house unting. Both houses are owned by very old women, both of whom were spiritual healers but no longer practice their craft.

Because Bananao has had electricity since 1997, 81 percent of the houses in Bayongyong have electricity. Only four houses in Bayongyong are without electricity, the owners saying they cannot afford it. Seldom are there more than one or two low-wattage light bulbs in a house. Some households have a television set—59 percent—even though they receive only one or two poor signals from the Cagayan Valley, and some of the sets do not work. Fifty-nine percent of the houses have a radio. A little over 20 percent of the households in Bayongyong have a small refrigerator; except for one family, any family that has a refrigerator also has a small *sari-sari* store (a small out-of-house store).

In Bananao, a few families still cook on a hearth with wood, but more and more families now are using propane gas stoves. In Bayongyong, 50 percent of the families cook exclusively with fuelwood, which they burn in their hearth. Children are a great help in gathering dead wood from the upper forests and uma, or from the river.

As in so many rural Philippine communities, water for drinking, washing clothes, and bathing is a constant concern. In Bananao, the upper part of the barangay receives water from a natural spring located a quarter of a kilometer above the community. The water flows into a storage tank, through rubber hose piping; both the tank and the piping were installed by the government. In the lower parts of Bananao, there are hand pumps, which operate most of the year. The residents go to the pumps and carry buckets of water back to their houses. With gravity-driven piped water, three of the households in Bayongyong have a sink in the kitchen area.

During the two- to three-month dry season, and when there is very little rain, the residents have to walk down to the Siffu River to bathe, wash clothes, and secure drinking water. There, they get the water for drinking just as their ancestors did—they dig a hole in the sandy soil at the riverbank and let fresh water seep upward. The culturally prescribed behavior for bathing has changed since the earlier study. In 1965, both males and females went down to the mountain stream and entered the water naked to bathe. Cultural modesty demanded that the bather back into the stream, covering his or her genitalia with one hand. Today, when the people of the area bathe in the river, modesty requires that men wear Western-style underwear or short pants and women wear short pants and a T-shirt or a dress.

There is no sewerage system in Bananao. Most toilet activity is taken care of in the privacy of the remote scrub brush areas of the community. Three households in Bayongyong, however, have an indoor toilet, which drains into an open area.

A general marker of contemporary wealth among rural Filipinos is the furnishings in the house. How much and how elaborate the furniture usually depend on the wealth of the family. Currently, small amounts of furniture are common in most, but not all, Ga'dang houses. If the family has a little wealth, there may be a *sala* set (a matching chair or two and a couch made from wood or bamboo) in the sitting room. Some families have an occasional chair or stool made from wood in the room. Food is often eaten in this room and a few families have a table for eating and maybe a wooden bench. In Bayongyong, 27 percent of the households have a sala set and/or a wooden bench.

In the 1965 study, almost all Ga'dang families had a granary in which they stored rice, located near the house or at the uma site. These granaries were very well constructed—more secure and leakproof than most houses. A granary was built up on three-foot pilings, the walls were made from woven bamboo, the thatching was tightly positioned, and the small door was secure. Round wooden guards encircled each support post to keep rats and other pests from crawling up the post into the granary. A family's rice for the whole year was stored in the granary, so security had to be of the highest priority.

Granaries as they existed in 1965–66 are now outdated. Most people use the inside of their house to store their grains, either rice, corn, or both. Where they do exist, they are constructed of planked boards and have a corrugated roof. The guards encircling the four posts on which the granary is constructed are usually made from five-gallon cooking-oil cans. As will be discussed later, upland rain-fed rice has become a minor crop in Bayongyong, so the need for a granary in which to store rice is less important to the Ga'dang of today. A few granaries are built in the mountain forests where most of the Ga'dang of Bayongyong still practice uma cultivation.

Chicken houses and chicken nests made from bamboo are as common today in the village as they were in 1965. While the Ga'dang in Bayongyong have not yet turned to raising their pigs in stalls or pens, the pigs are nonetheless usually tied so that they do not wander around the village. Many of the pigs now are crossbreeds between native Asian pigs and pig stock imported from the U.S. and Europe. Consequently, they are potentially more destructive to a village than the smaller native pigs of the past that were allowed to wander the village.

Because most of the households in Bayongyong still grow small amounts of upland rice in their uma located higher in the mountains, the traditional two-and-one-half-foot tall mortar for pounding rice to remove the chaff, with its accompanying four-foot-long pestle, are still found among the households. Hand-woven baskets in different sizes and shapes, formerly used for carrying foods from the field to the house, for storage, and for carrying things in general, are now uncommon. It was common for a man to carry a spear, especially if making a long trip. In those days, spears were used as weapons and they were a sign of manhood. Today, men do not carry spears but do wear a machete, at least when going to the fields to work. A few men wear the older, large machete (palatao) secured in a wooden scabbard, but most men now use commercially made machete that they keep in a leather casing. In 1965, an occasional head axe and numerous spears could be found stored in the houses. Today, such items are a thing of the past, most of them, like the old beads, having been sold to antique dealers.

Modernity on the Farm to Market Road

The Magat River serves as the boundary between the provinces of Isabela and Ifugao. To reach the Ga'dang from the Cagayan Valley side of the Cordillera Central in the 1960s and 1970s, it was necessary to cross the Magat River, and that was no easy task, especially during the rainy season. When the river was flowing, people crossed the river in small, pole-pushed boats. In the far north where the Magat River merges with the Cagayan River, a few motor-powered boats were available. Water buffalo and cattle swam the river, usually led by their owners who rode in the boat. At an area of the river between the small community of Ramon, Isabela, and the small community of Potia (now Alfonso Lista), Ifugao, there was a cable-pulled, flat-bottom, wooden barge, large enough to carry one small truck, a jeepney, a couple of motorcycles (although motorcycles did not enter the Cagayan Valley until 1966), or a few people. There was a dirt road, passable only when it was not raining, that extended from Potia toward Bayongyong, Paracelis, in Mountain Province. In 1966, the road did not extend all the way to Mountain Province.

There was no road between the Poblacion of Paracelis and Bananao in 1966. Access to the Ga'dang of the greater Paracelis area was usually accomplished by walking from the Cagayan Valley. The Ga'dang could also be reached by poling up the Siffu River from the Cagayan Valley, a full day's trip. The mountain people from Bontoc and Natonin would also walk down from higher elevations of the Cordillera Central to visit friends and search for land in Paracelis. The Ga'dang used the small Isabela communities of San Mateo and Roxas as centers in which to trade in 1965–66. Depending on their original location and the weather situation, this was a one- to four-day walk.

Paracelis, Mountain Province, was designated a distinct municipality in 1962 by the Philippine government. By the late 1960s, the dirt road from Potia was being extended closer to Mountain Province. The road from Tuguegarao in the Cagayan Valley to Tabuk, Kalinga, with a side-road to Paracelis was under construction. By late 1973, there was a dirt and gravel road extending all the way from Potia to Paracelis. It, however, was still only passable during the dry season. But, between the provinces of Ifugao and Isabela, there was still no way to cross the Magat River except by barge. In reality, the Ga'dang area was still cut off from the commercial centers of the Cagayan Valley because of the Magat River.

This changed in 1983. In 1983, a dam was constructed across the Magat River; at the time, it was the largest dam in Asia. There was now a farm–to-market road that extended from the commercial centers of Isabela trough Ifugao and into Mountain Province. The people of northern Ifugao and southern Mountain Province were able to interact with outsiders on a daily basis. Products from other parts of the Philippines easily entered the village of Bayongyong, and the products of the people of Bayongyong could easily be sent to the cities. Public buses and jeepneys were using the road with regularity by the 1990s. People could visit relatives in places like Baguio or Bontoc by riding in a bus for 12 hours rather than walking for three or four days up the mountains. Politicians, both elected and appointed, could visit rural areas and much more easily communicate with the people, creating a level of cooperation (and sometimes competition) never before seen in the mountains. The trip from Bayongyong to the Poblacion in Paracelis took only an hour by jeepney rather than the day it took to walk before the road was built. Convenient exposure to the Poblacion allowed Ga'dang families in Bananao to interact with political figures and government bureaucrats, the governmental educational system, and the medical system. In brief, the people living in previously isolated villages like Bayongyong became participating members of the greater Paracelis Municipality, with the benefits and challenges the road to modernization presented.

Today, the most common vehicle on the farm-to-market road in the area is the motorcycle. For example, in Bayongyong, 31 percent of the households own a motorcycle. One household owns an old Korean-made van, which the family occasionally uses as a commercial vehicle to transport people between Bananao and the Poblacion or the Cagayan Valley.

In the 1965–66 study, not a single Ga'dang household in Pakak or Cabanuangan owned a TV or even a battery-operated radio. With the arrival of electricity in 1997 the Ga'dang were exposed to the events of the Philippines and the rest of the world through television. Reception however, was limited to one, sometimes two, channels. It was common for people to visit their neighbors who owned a television to watch programs beamed into the area from one of the large towns in the Cagayan Valley. One family in Bayongyong owned a satellite dish but it did not work.

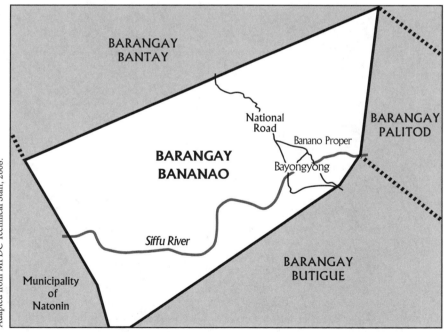

Barangay Bananao.

Chapter 4

Weeds and Corn
Environmental and Economic Change

$\mathcal{I}$n the 1965–66 study, while sitting in a mountain forest somewhere between Pakak and Bayongyong, an old Ga'dang woman said to me, "*Pekato-letam yo mula a ya'da na lubag ana yo lubag akanen detam.*" This roughly translates into English as "We eat the plants that the earth gives us and the earth eats us." Her understanding of human–nature relationships is a reminder that humanity and nature are interdependent parts of the whole. Humanity takes from nature, and in return, nature takes from humanity. In a harmonious world, there would be a balance in nature such that the human populations, and flora and fauna populations, would exist and die according to the laws of nature. Over the past hundred years, the equilibrium between humanity and nature has been dramatically disrupted through the acts of humanity—through deforestation, particularly in the tropical and semi-tropical regions of the world (Fujisaka et al. 1986; Wallace 2006). Humankind has taken too much from nature. This arresting shift in the balance of nature along the eastern slopes of the Cordillera Central and the Cagayan Valley stimulated dramatic changes in Ga'dang culture.

The Loss of Biodiversity

When the Spanish arrived in the Philippines in the sixteenth century, there were a few areas along the coastal areas that had been deforested along with the rice terracing areas of Northern Luzon. It has been estimated that at the time, somewhere between 80 and 95 percent of the Philippines was covered with old-growth rain forests, and the islands housed one of the most diverse flora and fauna populations in the world (cf. Heaney 1998; Kummer

51

1991; van den Top 2003). The native peoples of the Philippines, at least prior to the arrival of the Spanish, had not significantly modified their environment.

Even after 300 years of Spanish rule, around 70 percent of the land mass of the islands was covered by rain forest cover (Heaney 1998). Except for islands such as Cebu, where the Spanish dominated the countryside, much of the country was intact in its earlier environmental biodiversity. By the year 2000, however, the amount of rain forest cover had shrunk to around 7 percent, a drop of more than 60 percent in 100 years. This overwhelming trend in deforestation, and the loss of the biodiversity in the country, is one of the most dramatic in the world. The causes are many and complicated, but chief among them are population growth, agricultural expansion to feed a rapidly growing population, and illegal logging. The eastern slopes of the Cordillera Central and the Cagayan Valley, the homeland of the Ga'dang, have been environmentally devastated by these factors.

Figures detailing the population of the Ga'dang between 1903 (a few years after the Philippines became independent from the Spanish) and the present are not available. Importantly, however, the Ga'dang, based on my observations and discussions with older Ga'dang, as a minority population, had minimal influence on the changing environment of the area as compared to the other populations. The overall population structure for the area in which the Ga'dang lived or live as a minority, follows.

In 1903, soon after the Americans assumed oversight of the Philippines, the combined population of the provinces of Isabela, Cagayan, and Mountain Province—the basic areas where the Mountain Ga'dang had to compete for resources—was 378,586 (Philippine Census 1960). By 1960, the general population of these three provinces was 1,322,190, almost 3.5 times the population of 1903 (Philippine Census 1960). The resources of the forests for the Ga'dang were plentiful in 1903, but by 1960, the forests, except in the upper portions of the Cordillera, existed only as small pockets, often measuring no more than two or three square kilometers in size. This was the situation in 1965–66 during my initial Ga'dang study. By 2008, the general population in Isabela, Cagayan, and Mountain Province had grown to 4.5 million people, more than tripling the 1960 figures for the area (PNSO 2008). Because the rapidly expanding population claimed forest land for tobacco cultivation and drying, rice cultivation, illegal logging, fuelwood, and kaingin cultivation by pioneer and established farmers (Wallace 2006), by the time of the restudy, there were no forests remaining in the Ga'dang area except in the upper mountains in Ifugao and Mountain Province.

Between the 1965–66 study and the restudy, the environment of the Ga'dang was transformed from a mixed environment with pockets of forest reflecting a generalized ecosystem to a specialized ecosystem reflecting the handiwork of humanity. Most significantly, as noted earlier, in the environment of the Cagayan Valley and the eastern slopes of the Cordillera Central, the grass (*Imperata cylindrica*) commonly known as cogon but called akun by

A footpath through mature cogon, 1965.

the Ga'dang becomes the dominant replacement flora when an area is defor-ested. Except for use as thatching for houses, the grass is basically useless, and even more importantly, it is so tenacious and invasive (MacDonald 2004) that once it takes hold, it can choke out a rain-fed rice field in only a matter of two or three years. What was once a forest-covered landscape had become, by the time of the restudy, a sea of grass.

Making a Living in 1965–66

Two distinct Ga'dang farming systems were in operation in the 1965–66 study, one in Pakak, where the families were kaingin cultivators, and the other in Cabanuangan, where the families were plow farmers. Importantly, except in matters of economics, there were few cultural differences between the people of Pakak and Cabanuangan (cf. Wallace 1969, 1970). As noted

Uma Categories	Month	Activity
busing	February	site selection and preliminary cutting
pidwana busing	March	the second cutting
mataraw		trimming the trees
nauma		the uma is cut
magangu		the felled materials are drying
sikulan	May	burning the debris
makat		piling debris and reburning
malandak	June	pulling the weeds
makamel	July	cleaning the uma
mimunaw		a rice rite
mabini		planting the rice
mamula		planting the cultigens
mamuwawan	September	protecting the uma
magani	December	harvesting the rice
mamilag		drying the rice
madot		tying the rice into bundles
miudu		placing the rice in the granary

Figure 1   Uma Cultivation

earlier, the two Ga'dang communities had lived side by side in the same forest only a few years earlier.

The people of Pakak, traditional uma cultivators, divided the year into two seasons, "rice growing" and "other domesticated plant growing." The Pakak Ga'dang did not consider fallowing an integral step in uma cultivation. Unlike some other slash-and-burn cultivators who allowed kaingin sites to lie fallow after farming for only one to three years (cf. Conklin 1957; Dozier 1966; Freeman 1955; Geddes 1954), the Pakak Ga'dang chose to farm an uma for several years in succession. In their environment, overcultivating the land led to the rapid spread of cogon grass. As a result, when coupled with the activities of the pioneering cultivators, this led to deforestation and the loss of uma cultivatable land for the Ga'dang. I asked a Ga'dang man why he continued to cultivate his uma until the cogon choked out the rice. His response was simple. He said, "There is always a new forest to farm." As he and other Ga'dang were soon to discover, the forests and their edible resources would soon disappear.

The outcome of this cultural view of uma cultivation is illustrated by the yearly decline in rice yields. A survey of the uma in Pakak in 1965 revealed that rice yields, measured in cavans (which is equal to about 2.13 U.S. bushels), were highly dependent on the number of years rice was planted in succession in the uma. Based on a compilation of data, the average yields from a first, second, and third years' uma were as follows: first year—20 to 50 cavans per hectare, second year—15 to 30 cavans per hectare, and third year—10 to 20 cavans per hectare.

A second-year uma produced 50 percent less rice than was produced in a first-year uma. A third-year uma produced around than 50 percent of that produced in a second-year uma. It was not economic to cultivate an uma in Pakak for four years in succession. By then, the cogon grass had reduced the rice yield to almost nothing. A Pakak household in 1965 needed to prepare a new uma every three or four years. If suitable forestland were available nearby, the family would remain in Pakak. If land were not available, they would have to go to another forest.

During the rice-growing season, and during the other domesticated-plant-growing season, the Ga'dang planted numerous cultigens such as various kinds of beans, cowpeas, garlic, sponge gourd, fruit, and tomatoes to mention only a few, so that an uma was producing harvestable foodstuffs on a daily basis throughout the year. In brief, a Ga'dang uma was mimicking the biodiversity of a rain forest.

The Ga'dang living in Cabanuangan had abandoned uma cultivation in favor of plow farming by 1965–66. These Ga'dang divided the agricultural year into the corn-rice season and the tobacco season (see figures 2 and 3).

In 1965–66, the families living in Pakak supplemented their diet through collecting, hunting, and fishing, although the food from these activities was minimal compared to farming. Parts of the forest in Pakak were abandoned kaingins so some foods were available from these sources. Edible grubs and other insects were eaten when available. The value of hunting was mainly from birds killed. People often talked about hunting wild boar, but in reality, the numbers of wild boar were very limited. The most important supplementary food-generating activity of the Pakak Ga'dang was fishing. The river near the village was a plentiful source of numerous fish, frogs, and an assortment of crustaceans, which they used for home consumption.

Pakak income was further supplemented from the sale of small amounts of dried tobacco leaves, which were grown during the non-rice-growing season. Occasionally, the people would float bamboo down the river to the low-

Corn	Month	Rice	Month	Activity
matabas	April	matabas	April	cleaning the uma
maparagut		maparagut		harrowing
sikulan		sikulan		burning the debris
maraud		maradu		plowing
maparagut		maparagut		harrowing
		maradu		plowing
		maparagut		harrowing
mamula	May	mabini	June	planting
malamun	June	malamun	July	weeding
maradu		maradu		plowing
malamun	July	malamun	August	weeding
mamuwawan	September			field Protection
mabuwat	September	magani	October	harvesting

Figure 2   Plow Farming—Corn and Rice

Tobacco	Month	Activity
matabas	October	cleaning
maparagut		harrowing
sikulan		burning the debris
maradu		plowing
maparagut	November	harrowing
maradu		plowing
maparagut		harrowing
mamula	December	planting
maradu		plowing
maparagut	January	harrowing
malamun		weeding
maradu		plowing
magatu	February–March	harvesting

Figure 3   Plow Farming—Tobacco

lands to sell. They also sold rattan and cogon grass for cash to lowlanders. The most important supplementary economic activity, however, was generated by their water buffalo. The people of Pakak had no need for carabao as draft animals as they were uma cultivators, so they rented them to the lowlanders, and were usually paid in rice.

In Cabanuangan, the people had very few sources of income other than from farming. There was a small river nearby, but because of dynamite fishing by a larger population of Ga'dang and the Ilocano, the river provided few fish, frogs, or other edible forms of river life. Probably as a form of nostalgia for the days when they created an edible forest in their uma, rather than for any important economic value, many of the Ga'dang families in Cabanuangan planted cultigens in large tin cans.

Making a Living Now

Just as the Ga'dang area was changed from a generalized ecosystem to a specialized ecosystem between 1965 and the present, the economic lives of the Ga'dang in Bayongyong and Bananao also have been dramatically changed. The economy is now based on cash. As one Ga'dang man said, "We grow corn to buy rice!"

Two factors were major contributors to stimulating the changes in the economic system for the Bananao Ga'dang: corn and land reform. Corn (*Zea mays L.*) has long been an important crop in the Philippines (Reed 1963; Umali 1960); it is second in importance only to rice. In the Ga'dang area, the environment is favorable for corn growth, and corn is less time consuming to produce than rice. Corn does not require the creation or maintenance of paddy dikes, to control or confine excess water, or the production of seedbeds, which require a controlled environment for planting seedlings whose resulting plants are transplanted in the ground. Corn can be interspersed with other crops or rotated with such crops as rice and vegetables, and more importantly, it is the one crop that can compete, at least on the eastern slopes of the Cordillera Central, with cogon grass.

Most farms in the Philippines are small, averaging two hectares, and are managed by a single family engaged in subsistence production. The average amount of land farmed by the Ga'dang in Bananao—land titled with the government and land not titled with the government but used through tradition—is 3.02 hectares. This is much more than the national average. The figure is skewed because the first Ga'dang family that settled in Bananao managed to title almost nine hectares of land. In Bayongyong, the average

Working in the uma, 1966 *(top)*.
Plowing and planting corn in Bayongyong, 2011 *(bottom)*.

amount of land devoted to corn is 2.24 hectares per household (some on titled land and some on untitled land). The largest amount of land devoted to corn by a household is seven hectares. The least amount of land devoted to corn is one-half hectare.

The actual steps in growing the corn in Bayongyong differs little from the procedures described for Cabanuangan 45 years ago (see figure 2): basically, cleaning (*matabas*), plowing (*maradu*), harrowing (*maparagut*), planting (*mabini*), weeding (*malamun*), and harvesting (*mabuwat*). The major difference now is there are two crops of corn a year (mainly field corn); the farmers now use commercial fertilizers, pesticides, and herbicides; and the plowing may be done with a mechanically powered plow or hand tractor. While there are still many carabao in use in Bayongyong, the hand tractor is starting to replace this traditional draft animal. The first corn season is from May to September; the second is from October to March.

In Bayongyong, the farmers harvest an average of 40 to 50 cavans of field corn per hectare for each of two crops a year. The economics of corn farming is tricky, especially if the household farms less than four hectares each year. Considering the cost of plowing, seeds, pesticides, weed killer, labor, harvesting, milling, and moving the crop to market, corn is expensive to grow. In Bayongyong, the cost of producing one hectare of corn is 75 percent of the sale price. With a household planting an average of 2.4 hectares in corn, the sale of the corn, even with two crops a year, is not sufficient to purchase rice for a year. When farmers were asked why they grow corn rather than rice, the general response was "the cogon chokes the rice." Consequently, the people of Bayongyong must find additional ways to make a living during the year.

Monsanto's Bt corn, genetically modified to be high-yielding and corn-borer resistant, has not reached Bananao yet, although it was introduced in 2003 in nearby Ifugao and is being used by a few farmers there, mainly when they are late in starting their crop (Bagyan and Gimenez 2005). The farmers of Bayongyong have no immediate plans to switch to Bt corn, although controlled trials elsewhere suggest the yields are twice to three times the yields of the seed currently being used (Yorobe and Quicoy 2006) by the Ga'dang. They have heard rumors about Bt's high cost of production, cross-pollination with other strains of corn, and problems it may cause cattle who consume it. It is, however, a current topic of discussion among some of the Ga'dang farmers. Their awareness of modern agricultural technologies, however, demonstrates that the Ga'dang are oriented toward the future rather than the past.

The more economically secure families in Bananao, which means families with more land, often have a symbiotic economic relationship with poor families, or families farming less than two hectares of land. The wealthier families will loan money to the poor families at a 20 percent interest rate for six months. The poor families borrow the money for two growing seasons a year and repay the debt in cash twice a year at harvest. With the money from the loan, the poor family must purchase seeds, pesticides, herbicides, and fertilizers from the same family that loaned them the money. Due to the 20 percent interest, the price to the poor family for these farming inputs is higher than the cost at the commercial centers in the Cagayan Valley. Regardless of the price of corn at the market, the wealthy family receives its loan repayment plus the 20 percent interest. In addition, of course, the family has already made a profit by selling the poor family the farm inputs. In many respects, the poor family can never accumulate enough capital to get out of debt. A variation of this type of debtor service is common throughout Northern Luzon.

As previously noted, another moneymaking enterprise is carabao rental. To a person unfamiliar with the rural Philippines, purchasing and owning a carabao may not seem significant. Nevertheless, the ability to purchase a carabao is noteworthy, considering the average day wage in northern Luzon is 200 pesos a day and a trained, mature carabao may cost as much as 30,000 pesos or 150 days of day labor. In the Bananao region, the day labor wage is as low as 130 pesos a day. At this rate, it would take a person 200 days of day labor to purchase one carabao. Simply stated, purchasing a carabao is impossible for most Ga'dang without another source of income. They may receive additional income in the form of cash from owning a large amount of land that produces crops they can sell at a profit; from children who have moved to the larger cities, secured a well-paying job, and send part of their earnings home; or in a few cases, from a relative who is working as a domestic in another country such as Saudi Arabia. Once owned by a family, a carabao provides further income because the family can rent it to poor farmers who cannot afford to purchase their own.

As noted, most Bayongyong families, since they only have an average of a little over two hectares of land, must create supplemental income in order to buy rice for the year. To supplement their income, the Ga'dang have returned to their tradition of uma cultivation. While slash-and-burn cultivation by the Ga'dang in Bayongyong remains fundamentally as it was during the 1965–66 study (see figure 1), there have been some significant changes, the most significant of which is the uma is cultivated for only one season a year. The land is allowed to lie fallow for about six months a year. The reasons for this are clear: (1) the farmers now perceive land as being privately owned as opposed to pressing it through usufruct rights, and (2) the farmers accept that there are no more forests to cultivate so they must protect what little uma land they farm.

A cultural practice that has been eliminated by the Ga'dang is no longer following the taboos when selecting an uma site—such as if a man sees a snake hanging from a tree, a kingfisher crosses his path, or he hears a deer calling, he will look elsewhere for a site. There is no longer a rice ritual associated with planting or harvesting the rice. The Ga'dang still believe, however, that upland rice must be planted using a digging stick; otherwise, the taste of the rice will be bitter and the yield may be low.

Although upland rice, harvested and processed by hand with a traditional mortar and pestle brings a higher price in the lowland markets, the Ga'dang grow rice in their uma for home consumption. In all cases, the uma of the Bananao Ga'dang are located higher in the mountains west and south-west of the barangay. Depending on a person's capabilities and the exact location of the field, it takes anywhere from one to two hours to hike to the uma from the village. (During the earlier study, the swiddens were seldom more than 15 minutes from the location of the family's house.) Forty-seven percent of the Ga'dang households in Bananao maintain an uma in the mountains, almost all of it on untitled land but perceived by the Ga'dang as usufruct land with inheritance rights. Approximately 23 percent of the Bayongyong Ga'dang maintain their uma in the mountains.

A Ga'dang uma today is more uniform in size than it was during the earlier study. In 1965–66, the size of a swidden plot varied anywhere from 300 or 400 square meters up to one hectare or 10,000 square meters. Today, the mountain swidden plots are consistently between one-half and one hectare. The yields for upland rice now are much the same as they were for a second or third year uma in the 1965 study because the land is fallowed and plants regenerate during the six months of cultivation inactivity.

Cultigens other than rice are grown in the uma, but the varieties of edible foods are limited as compared to Ga'dang uma of the 1960s. In the past, between 20 to 25 different cultigens could be found growing in an uma during certain times of the year. This is not a large number compared to other swidden cultivating societies (e.g. Conklin 1957; Spencer 1966), but it is a much greater variety than can be found in contemporary Ga'dang uma, where only six or seven cultigens are grown.

Since the Ga'dang of the Bananao area are fundamentally permanent field farmers who depend on cash, and because many of them or their parents moved to the area in the late 1960s or early 1970s, some more permanent crops are well established in the area. For example, coconut and betel nut palms are a feature of the landscape, as are several varieties of bananas. The fruits of the coconut and betel nut palms are mainly for home consumption. Bananas are consumed at home, but they are also sold.

During the uma season—generally April to November—the families of Bayongyong spend considerable time working in the uma. Because the swiddens are cultivated yearly, there are no large trees to be felled, but the area still must be cleared, burned, and cleaned again, planted, protected, and harvested. The men usually do the clearing and burning, while men, women and children are involved in planting, weeding, and harvesting. Protection of the uma, especially from birds as the grain ripens, is a necessary and time-consuming activity. Many of the households in Bayongyong construct a small, makeshift house in the uma during this critical period so someone from the family can stay there for several days at a time. In the 1960s, a network of upright bamboo poles connected by strips of rattan could be manipulated so that a loud clapping sound was created, which frightened the birds away. This apparatus is not present in the swiddens of the people of Bayongyong today.

Making a living for the people of Bayongyong requires ingenuity and diligence, but by maintaining a small uma, growing and selling corn, working as day laborers for wealthy farmers along the road, doing a little fishing, and often getting little monetary help from children or other relatives working for cash in the cities, the Mountain Ga'dang live much like most other rural and poor Filipinos. Some of the Ga'dang with larger land holdings, or with more money coming in from outside, can support a more comfortable lifestyle. As noted earlier, a few families have luxuries such as a television, a refrigerator, a motorcycle, and perhaps even a truck.

In addition to the importance of a changing environment forcing the Mountain Ga'dang to participate in a cash economy, the most significant event conditioning the economic life of the communities was land reform. Obtaining and retaining title to land has been a serious problem for poor and/or landless Filipinos since the days of the Spanish and the early U.S. administration. In particular, the indigenous peoples of the Cordillera Central have been caught in a legal contradiction since the Land Registration Act of 1902, which required the acquisition of a Torrens title as proof of land owner- ship, and the Public Land Act of 1905, which declared all unregistered lands and those without Torrens title to be public lands (see Crisologo-Mendoza and Prill-Brett 2009). At the time, the people of the Cordillera were occupy- ing and using forestlands based on culturally interpreted usufruct rights to gather, hunt, fish, and cultivate. Conversely, in 1950, an Executive Order was issued that gave indigenous people the right to acquire titles over lands they had occupied and cultivated within the Central Cordillera Forest Reserve.

These laws, one taking the lands away from them by declaring that their indigenous territory was forest reserve (public lands) and the other giving indigenous peoples the right to title land that they had occupied throughout their known history, were contradictory. To complicate matters more, a 1978 presidential decree declared all people who occupied public forestlands as squatters subject to ejection and relocation by the government. To this day, the contradictions in Philippine laws regarding public lands, land tenure, land titles, and indigenous rights remain in a legal state subject to numerous inter- pretations. Even though the Philippines has been in the forefront of the fight for the rights of indigenous peoples in Southeast Asia, and the Philippine Indigenous Peoples Rights Act was signed into law in 1997 (Republic of the Philippines 1997), claims and counterclaims continue to create friction within tribal groups, between tribal groups, and between tribal groups and the Philippine government.

Many of the Ga'dang in the greater Paracelis area started taking advan- tage of the Executive Order of 1950 that gave indigenous people the right to acquire title to land they had occupied and cultivated. As the forest started to disappear, and people started to migrate to the Bananao area, the few Ga'dang families that were already living in the area in the late 1950s began filing for title to the land they had been cultivating. Because the law allows the land to be legally inherited, today a few Ga'dang families in Bananao have as much as six or seven hectares of titled land, much more than the national average. The descendents of the first Ga'dang man to settle in Bayongyong have a little more than eight hectares of titled land. This amount of titled land, however, is very unusual. The average titled land holdings for the Ga'dang in the Bananao area is only 1.3 hectares. Families who arrived later or who had no relatives in the area, many from the areas of my 1965–66 study, have much smaller titled land holdings.

Exploring what constitutes "quality of life" in society (see Veenhoven 2006, 2010) is for another venue, but if the quality of life for a population is measured only in terms of the availability, variety, and quality of native foods, a comparison between 1965–66 and the present shows that most Ga'dang have a diet, except for the variety of vegetables, similar to what they had almost 50 years ago. Since the economy of today is based on cash, however, Ga'dang with more wealth in Bananao have access to more commercial foods (such as canned sardines, canned meat, dried fish, breads, and candies or snack foods). They purchase these goods either in town or at a neighborhood sari-sari store. Bayongyong has three of these small variety home-based stores, which sell items such as canned goods, soft drinks, candies, salt, sugar, and cigarettes.

A comparison of the types and frequency of foods eaten (if in season) by the people in Pakak in 1965–66 and the people of Bayongyong in 2011 is found in figure 4. The comparison of foods consumed by the Ga'dang in 1965–66 and the present reflects only when the foods were available or in season. For example, in Pakak, wing beans were eaten three times a day when in season. During the remainder of the year, there were no wing beans to eat.

Comparing the foods eaten by the Ga'dang during the 1965–66 study and what they eat now suggests that most of the differences are a result of the changing environment. For example, the Ga'dang in Bayongyong do not eat monkey, fruit bat, wild chicken, wild duck, green pigeon, wing beans, and millet because these foods are not available in the area. The Ga'dang in Pakak did not eat polished or white rice because they grew enough upland rice to feed the household for the year. Difficult to locate or expensive animals such as carabao, wild boar, pig, and deer were seldom eaten in the 1960s, and that remains so today. The river near Pakak clearly provided access to more fresh water foods than the Siffu River provides for the inhabitants of Bayongyong. The Ga'dang in Bayongyong make use of the local sari-sari stores, while the Ga'dang living in Pakak and Cabanuangan had to walk for a day to reach a store.

Potential Foods	Pakak, 1965–66	Bayongyong, 2010–11
carabao (*dafug*)	1 time a year	1 time a year
wild boar (*bafui natatun*)	1 time a year	1 time a year
domestic pig (*bafui*)	1 time a year	1 time a year
deer (*uta*)	1 time a year	1 time a year
dog (*atu*)	1 time a year	3 times a year
fruit bat (*paniki*)	2 times a year	0 times a year
monkey (*uwao*)	1 time a year	0 times a year
chicken (*manuk*)	2 times a month	1 time a week
chicken egg (*ilug*)	2 times a month	1 time a week
wild chicken (*gitalun*)	2 times a year	0 times a year
green pigeon (*funai*)	1 time a month	0 times a year
dove (*balug*)	1 time a month	0 times a year
maya bird (*dinat*)	1 time a month	4 times a year
pigeon (*gurok*)	1 time a month	0 times a year
wild duck (*papa*)	1 time a year	0 times a year
mudfish (*dalug*)	1 time a month	1 time a month
catfish (*patat*)	1 time a month	1 time a year
carp (*burasi*)	1 time a week	2 times a year
sharkfish (*kukirao*)	1 time a month	0 times a year
crawfish (*paiyan*)	1 time a month	0 times a year
fresh water crab (*amaa*)	3 times a week	3 times a week
snail (*urung*)	1 time a month	2 times a week
fresh water shrimp (*ladao*)	1 time a day	2 times a week
uma rice (*apai*)	3 times a day	3 times a day
white rice (*apai*)	0 times a day	3 times a day
millet (*nana*)	3 times a month	0 times a year
camote (*gasilung*)	1 time a day	2 times a week
camote leaves (*singafui*)	1 time a day	2 times a week
eggplant (*balinsioa*)	3 times a day	3 times a day
onion (*dangu*)	2 times a day	2 times day
wing beans (*buligan*)	3 times a day	0 times a year
lima beans (*bitag*)	3 times a day	2 times a week
mungo beans (*balatung*)	2 times a day	1 time a week
corn (*bakao*)	0 times a year	1 time a day
bananas (*abat*)	1 time a day	1 time a day
sari-sari foods	0 times a week	4 times a week

Figure 4   A Comparison of Foods Eaten

Chapter 5

When a House
Is Not a Home

Social Change

$\mathcal{M}$easuring change in some cultural domains is less problematic than measuring change in other domains. For example, the Ga'dang economic system can be measured with more quantification than, for example, the Ga'dang "concept of self." Changes in the environment on the eastern slopes of the Cordillera Central can be observed and measured because the forests of the area were replaced by cogon grass and then by corn. These types of change are observable and measurable. The economy of the Pakak Ga'dang was based on uma cultivation while the economy of the Bananao Ga'dang is based on cash. This type of culture change can be measured with few ambiguities, both quantifiably and qualitatively. The addition of a material item, such as a cell phone, a motorcycle, or a pair of shoes, to a culture is a straightforward measure of change. The absence of a cultural item, such as traditional attire or a head axe, is a simple measure of change. Identifying and then measuring change in the cultural domains of social life and spiritual life, however, becomes more problematic and more difficult to do with a high degree of confidence.

In this chapter, I examine the changes that have occurred in the social life of the Ga'dang from 1965–66 to the present and show how these changes are affecting the actions of both old and young people in the Bananao area. Measuring culture change in the spiritual realm of life will be examined in later chapters.

Growing Up Ga'dang

During the 1965–66 study, birth was an event that occurred at home, usually with the aid of a female shaman/medium (makamong) who had learned the skills of midwifery through experience. If a midwife was not available, a female relative or the husband would help with the birth. All children born during the earlier study were born in the house in which they lived or a nearby house. In some cases, the mother gave birth lying on her back, and in other cases, she gave birth while squatting. As soon as the child was born, it was washed, wrapped in a cloth, and both the child and the mother were given small amounts of a tea made from herbs found in the forest. The placenta carried no cultural significance and was either thrown away or buried. If the child died before naming, it was quickly buried in the nearby forest. If the child survived, it received its name, usually taken from an ancestor, three days after birth. If the child was a boy, the name was usually that of a father's father, if a girl, a mother's mother. Occasionally, a child would be named after the sound made by an animal or after a plant. The child received only one name. A small and brief naming ritual was performed for the household by a makamong. She received a chicken for her services. For five months after birth, the mother was prohibited from eating sugarcane, fish killed by dynamite, or jackfruit. If she broke this taboo, she could go into a trance and die.

Currently, Ga'dang women still give birth in the home or in a nearby home. Instead of being aided by a makamong, however, she is helped by a formally trained midwife, a *mafuyat*. In Bananao, there are two mafuyat. Both midwives in Bananao received a four-day, intensive training course taught by nurses in the Poblacion of Paracelis. The course was sponsored by the Philippine government and included lessons on how to care for an expectant mother and how to identify potential problems the expectant mother might encounter. If the midwife anticipates that there may be problems for the mother or the child, she will arrange to get a physician to visit the expectant mother in her home. Both midwives in Bananao already had some experience in helping women give birth before they received their formal training. The mother of one of the midwives had been a makamong. For helping with the birth, the midwife is given a donation. Usually this is in the form of a small amount of money, but more often, she is given some rice or a chicken.

The actual act of giving birth is much the same today as it was in the past. Today, however, after the child is washed and wrapped in a cloth, the mother and child are given some antibiotics and a tea made from pineapple suckers and ginger. In addition, both the mother and child are given a small amount of San Miguel Ginebra gin to help the "blood circulate." The new mothers in Bananao no longer follow the food taboos of the past.

Naming a child is markedly different today than it was 45 years ago. The Ga'dang live in a modernizing world, and if they are going to participate fully in this world, they must follow the laws of The Family Code of the Philippines (Executive Order 1987). This code affects most levels of family life in

A mother with children, 1966 *(top)*.
Two mothers with children, 2010 *(bottom)*.

the Philippines: naming, marriage, divorce, property rights, inheritance, and death. All Ga'dang children born now in Bananao must be registered with the Philippine government. They must have both a first name and a surname. Their parents must be identified. Otherwise, effectively they do not legally exist and are not entitled to the rights and privileges of being a Philippine citizen. This is particularly important today for the Ga'dang because they have become permanent field farmers. The inheritance of land is critical to family survival. This was not an important issue for the Ga'dang of the past since they moved every few years.

Today, people know their date of birth because the law has made a person's date of birth a relevant legal and cultural category. Most Ga'dang over the age of 40, however, do not know their actual date of birth. In fact, most of them do not know the year in which they were born. People over 40, however, do usually know the place where they were born because their parents told them the location. As with a surname, date of birth did not become important until the inheritance of property became a critical cultural category.

As titled land became increasingly more important to the Ga'dang, most of the men and women who did not have a surname began to register with the Philippine government. This meant they had to have a surname, so what they tended to do was use their Ga'dang name as the surname and add a first name, or keep their Ga'dang name as the first name, and either invent a surname or take a surname from anyone who was well-known in the area. What mattered was that they were registered.

There have been few changes in the manner in which parents interact with their children since 1965, especially during early childhood. Much of the first two years of life for the child is spent in a hip sling. A child's mother or father, mainly the mother, will carry the child in the hip sling almost everywhere she goes throughout the day. The child is with her when she is cooking, washing, or working in the field. The child is given the mother's breast any time he or she feels hungry. If there are no younger children, the child is allowed to suck almost at will until the age of three, and sometimes four. It is unusual for a mother to play with a child by tickling, gently poking, or blowing on some part of the child's body. The mother shows affection to the child by gently stroking the child and by picking lice from the child's head. Little attempt is made to "potty" train the child. Infants and young children seldom wear diapers or underpants. If a parent senses a child needs to urinate or defecate, the mother or father will take the child by the arms and hold the child out the door or window.

Between the ages of about three and six, children generally follow their mother or father around the village or to the fields, and learn to be young Ga'dang. Often, older siblings guide the younger child through this stage of life. Little girls mimic the behavior of mothers and little boys mimic the behavior of fathers. Children are seldom punished for misbehavior, although they may be scolded for a breach of social etiquette such as reaching in front of an adult for food during a meal. As one young Ga'dang woman said, "You cannot make a child do what he does not want."

The major difference in the life of a child between the 1965–66 study and the restudy is in formal education. No child in Pakak or Cabanuangan was attending school during the 1965–66 study. Children were not encouraged to attend school because there were no schools in the immediate vicinity.

The first elementary school was established in Bananao (Butigue) in 1959. The school was a one-room bamboo house, and the teacher was a Balangao man from Natonin who married a Ga'dang woman. According to his daughter, the current head teacher in the original Bananao elementary school, her father had a total of 12 students for the first few years of his operation, all of whom were at least ten years old when they started school.

The elementary school (kindergarten through grade six) has grown considerably since its early days. The school is in its same location but now consists of three cement block buildings and one bamboo-wood kindergarten building, housing six classrooms and a teacher's room/office. The school has seven teachers, one for each grade. One teacher is from a Balangao/Ga'dang family and the others are Ilocano. Theoretically, subjects are taught in Pilipino (effectively Tagalog) and English. In reality, most education is carried out in Ilocano because it is the lingua franca of the area, and children grow up speaking Ilocano even if their parent's original language is Ga'dang, Balangao, Ifugao, or something else.

The Philippine Department of Education cannot keep pace with the needs of a rapidly growing school-age Filipino population. For example, the Bananao elementary school has no computers, and teachers say that they have only 20 percent of the books they need. These are books required by the Philippine curriculum. Enrollment figures for this Bananao elementary school are, as follows:

Year	No. of Students
2010–2011	165
2009–2010	150
2008–2009	173
2007–2008	172
2006–2007	230

According to the teachers, enrollments have been steady for a decade or so in Bananao Elementary. The significant drop in enrollment in 2006–2007 and 2007–2008 was because a new elementary school (called an annex school) was constructed in a distant barangay of Bananao to serve the children on the other side of Bananao. Formerly, these children had to walk an hour to get to the Bananao school.

Based on my observations, the behavior among the students and the interaction with their teachers appear typical based on my years of visiting schools in the Philippines. The children are taught to be polite in class and always welcome the teacher in unison with a "Good Morning M. . . ." The principle underlying the education system appears to be based on how to memorize rather than on how to reason and think. In Bananao, the students leave their shoes, usually flip-flops, outside the classroom before entering. The parents of the students lobbied the teachers not to require school uniforms. Their argument was that many of the families could not afford the two uniforms required by the Department of Education.

In addition to inadequate facilities and books, the teachers believe that the biggest deterrent to a good education is the overall poverty of the local families (of course with a few exceptions). Absenteeism, especially among boys, is a definite problem. During planting and during the application of insecticides and herbicides to the corn, child labor is common, both within the family and as day laborers working outside of the family. For example, on the opening day of school in 2011, I was observing a two-hectare area of land that was being planted in corn. In this one area, I saw three Ga'dang elementary-school-age children working as day laborers. When I asked why they were not in school, I was told that the family needed the money.

Today in Bayongyong, only one person over the age of 60 ever attended high school, and he spent his high school years in the Poblacion. Three Ga'dang men, between the ages of 50 and 60, attended elementary school for a few years. These men were born to the early settlers in the Bananao area. Ga'dang between the ages of 40 and 50 have on average an elementary education. Most Ga'dang under the age of 40 have at least an elementary education, and many of them attended high school. Many Ga'dang under the age of 30 attended high school, although not all of them graduated. Today, teenagers attend high school regularly, and there have been a few Ga'dang from Bayongyong who have attended local collages located in Ifugao and Isabela. In the Philippines, a high school degree means that the student has completed the tenth grade (rather than twelve grades, although the Philippine government is discussing making some adjustments in the current grade structure).

During the 1965–66 study, all Ga'dang men spoke Ga'dang and Ilocano, and a few Ga'dang women were learning Ilocano. Today, all Ga'dang men, most women, and children speak Ga'dang and Ilocano. English is spoken by Ga'dang who attended school, especially high school, although there is considerable variation in vocabulary use. Ga'dang women over the age of 65 have very limited knowledge of English and sometimes have to struggle with Ilocano. If the household is composed of a Ga'dang wife and a Balangao husband, for example, the child will learn both Ga'dang and Balangao. Importantly, since Ilocano is the lingua franca of the area, Ilocano is spoken in the community as frequently as Ga'dang. During the restudy, when interviewing younger Ga'dang, I sometimes had to ask my questions in Ilocano rather than in Ga'dang. Younger Ga'dang speak Ga'dang, but especially in certain cultural domains, they occasionally are more knowledgeable in Ilocano.

As noted, when a Ga'dang child enters elementary school, he or she must know some Ilocano because although officially the language of elementary school is Pilipino (Tagalog), thus far, all teachers in the elementary school in Bananao have been Ilocano and/or Ga'dang speakers, and as in most rural areas in the Philippines, the teachers tend to teach in their most comfortable

A student prepares for school, 2011.

language. It is not that the teachers resist teaching in Pilipino, it is simply easier to teach in their native language and in the most commonly used language
in the area. The teachers, however, do carry out the language exercises in English and Pilipino required by the school system. Nevertheless, once the child
starts school, he or she spends more time speaking Ilocano than Ga'dang or
Pilipino. Ilocano is reinforced because the Ga'dang children attend school
with Ilocano, Ifugao, Balangao, and other language speakers so as a group of
children, they use the lingua franca of the area. The Philippine educational
system starts teaching English early in elementary school, so the Ga'dang
child also must deal with a third or fourth language. Consequently, any student with at least an elementary school education will probably speak the
native language of their parents, Ilocano, Pilipino, and perhaps some English.
The higher their grade level, the more fluent they are in Pilipino and English.

A high school—grades seven through ten—consisting of three bamboo
buildings housing four classrooms was formally established in the barangay

of Bananao in 2010. The campus was actually established as an annex school of barangay Butigue in 2006. Prior to 2006, high school students living in Bananao had to walk an hour or more to attend high school in the barangay of Butigue, which was established in 1984. Prior to 1984, the only high school in the vicinity was in the Poblacion of Paracelis, a trip too far and too expensive for a daily commute. Students from the Bananao area who attended high school there either lived with relatives or rented floor space on which to sleep.

The year the new school was formally opened, the bamboo structures were demolished, and two cement block buildings containing three classrooms each were constructed. Currently, there are seven teachers, five permanent (paid by the Department of Education) and two temporary (paid from municipal funds). There is one teacher of English, one math teacher, one science teacher, one technology and livelihood (agriculture and home economics) teacher, one teacher of Pilipino language and literature, and two history and social science teachers. The students receive one hour of instruction each day in the prescribed subject areas.

In March 2010, the Philippine Department of Education issued the new high school 11 computers, three printers, and a satellite dish to receive the Internet. As in many bureaucracies, however, the new equipment did not include funds for maintenance, and in the case here, there were no funds allocated for printer ink and paper. The students are not allowed to use school computers for personal correspondence through such instruments as Facebook or e-mail. And, with a school enrollment of 186 students in four grades and only ten computers (as one must function as the server), computer-use time for the students is very limited.

In the formal shift from an annex high school to a national high school, some records were misplaced, so dropout figures are available only for 2010–11. During this year, out of 97 male and 89 female students, 11 males and 13 females dropped out of school. That is, there was an 11 percent dropout rate for males and a 14.6 percent dropout rate for females. There is no noticeable difference in dropout rates by ethnicity in Bananao. In addition, 13 males (13 percent) and four females (less than 1 percent) failed the year.

The numbers for Bananao are better than the national average.

> For every one hundred pupils who enter Grade 1, only eighty-six will go on to Grade 2. By Grade 4, only seventy-six of the original one hundred will still be in school. By Grade 6, only sixty-seven will still be enrolled— and only sixty-five will graduate from elementary school. Of the sixty-five who finish grade school, only fifty-eight will move on to high school. And of the fifty-eight who enter high school, only forty-two will graduate. (Gatbonton 2010)

In an attempt to gain a more clear appreciation for the ways Ga'dang youth perceive their future, a short survey dealing with the future and with students who dropped out of school was administered to 30 young Ga'dang, all from Bayongyong. There were two groups divided equally by age and by sex: males and females ages 10 to 15, and males and females ages 16 to 21.

Twenty-six percent of Bayongyong boys in the survey dropped out of elementary school. No girls in the survey dropped out of elementary school. Thirty-three percent of the boys interviewed dropped out of high school. Thirteen percent of the girls in the survey dropped out of high school. Nationally, the most vulnerable time for students to leave school is immediately after the first grade and during the seventh and eighth grades (Gatbonton 2010).

The most common reason given by boys for dropping out of school was poverty. The girls who dropped out of school expressed different reasons. Some brief statements from students who dropped out of school follow:

> "I decided to stop school because my parents cannot afford my needs in school." —A 16-year-old boy who dropped out of school in fourth grade.

> "I dropped out of school because my parents cannot support me because my father is always drinking alcohol, and there was only my mother to work the uma. I had to stop school to help her work the uma." —A 15-year-old boy who dropped out of school in the third grade.

> "I dropped from school in grade two because we were living in the fields and I am too lazy to walk two hours to school." —A 13-year-old boy who dropped out of school in second grade.

> "I dropped out of school because I got married at age 14." —A 21-year-old woman with two children.

> "I dropped out because of the temptation in life. I am repenting now." —A 19-year-old woman who dropped out of college in her first year.

For Ga'dang students still in school, there is a consistent theme: "I want to finish my studies." The following quote from a student in her last year of high school summarizes the positive attitude held by many young Ga'dang regarding the importance of education:

> My future plans in life are many, but first of all, I would like to finish my studies. I want to become a good lawyer because someday I want to serve my people, especially those poor people who cannot afford to fight for their human rights. I observed and experienced with my parents because they do not know how to fight for their rights. The problem is their lack of knowledge—even when they are in the right way.

Although this young Ga'dang woman is from a poor family, her mother is currently working as a domestic abroad so she can occasionally send money to her daughter to help with her education.

Courtship and Marriage

Traditionally and during the 1965–66 study, Ga'dang marriage was fundamentally about forming alliances between two families. The majority of girls were married by the age of 12 or 14, although the marriage was not consummated until after the girls reached puberty. Since a young man and woman received part of their inheritance at marriage, a family attempted to obtain for their son or daughter a mate who would contribute at least as much wealth to the new household as he or she would contribute. This inheritance generally consisted of pigs, carabao, beads, clothing, and rice. A young man, usually between the ages of 14 and 20, would inform his parents that he was interested in getting married. If the boy had not already selected a girl, his parents would help him find a suitable mate. If a young girl was already pregnant, her parents would start to look for a suitable husband, ideally the boy who was the father of her child to be.

Courtship as perceived in the Western world was not a relevant cultural category for the Ga'dang in 1965. If parents found a possible mate for a son or daughter, a go-between assumed the responsibility of negotiating a marriage between the two families. The go-between, always a man, because of his position of trust, negotiated a fair arrangement for both the boy's parents and the girl's parents. Once the marriage arrangements had been agreed upon, the boy's parents would present to the parents of the girl a single bead of considerable value—a kiring. A kiring was a bead of Spanish or Chinese origin, had been passed from generation to generation, and had the value of one carabao, sometimes more. If the girl had not passed puberty, the marriage would be delayed until that time and the kiring would be held in escrow until the marriage actually took place. If the boy's parents canceled the marriage, they would forfeit the kiring; if the girl's parents canceled, they would return it to the parents of the boy.

A man could take a wife from his own village, as long as it was not a first or second cousin, but usually, he took a wife from outside his local settlement. As one man said, "It is a good idea to get a wife from another part of the Ga'dang area. You will have relatives in different places. This allows you to go and visit different places. You will be safe there. A relative must help you when you come to visit." During the 1960s, the Ga'dang used whatever social means available to increase their network of kin. It was still a time of general fear of people who were not Ga'dang. The days of head taking were still fresh in the minds of many of the older Ga'dang.

The marriage ceremony (*pisel*) was an important social affair where relatives and friends of the principals and their parents came from nearby and distant communities. The boy's parents financed the event, it was held at their home, it lasted two days and one night, and it was officiated by a female medium (makamong) and a male medium (mabayen).

During the first day of the marriage ceremony, the boy's parents and their immediate kin prepared large quantities of food. A pig was brought to the house for the makamong and mabayen to inspect before it was killed. Large amounts of sugarcane wine and cheap, commercially produced gin were available for all the guests. The pig was killed by the male medium, but it was the female medium who had the responsibility of interpreting the sounds of the pig. It was she who had the power to postpone the ceremony if the signs were bad. As more and more guests began to arrive during the afternoon, the gaiety increased and more and more drink was consumed by the men, and some women. The mediums were praying and singing to ensure a good marriage with many children. Young men played games such as high jumping and broad jumping. The couple getting married took an active part in the festivities of the day.

Soon after dark, food was served and more drink was consumed. The men took out their gongs and began to play. Social dancing was the activity of the evening, with the couple to be married figuring prominently in the dancing activities. Sometime during the night, when the gong playing was at its loudest, and the dancing was at its fastest, the young couple would slip away to some unoccupied house where they would spend the night. The couple returned in the morning as man and wife. By the afternoon, the guests started to return to their homes.

For the first year of marriage, the couple tended, although it was not prescribed, to live in the village of the girl's parents. In effect, living in the village of the bride's parents was fulfillment of a bride service commitment the groom owed the parents of his bride. The newly married couple, however, built their own house and farmed their own fields. After a year, the couple might decide to move to a new village, depending on personal taste and economic opportunities.

If a betrothed couple were still children, the ceremony would not be held until the girl had passed puberty. If the girl had not yet passed puberty and the man was older, she might live in his house, but the marriage ceremony and consummation of the marriage would not take place until the girl reached puberty.

Divorce was easy, as it involved little more than the couple agreeing to separate and go their own way. The most common reasons for a divorce were (1) if either the husband or the wife was unwell or unable to provide food and clothing for his or her spouse, (2) if either the husband or the wife had a sexual relationship with another person without the permission of his or her spouse, (3) if either person should become a thief, and (4) if the parents of the couple had disagreements so strong that the community was seriously disrupted. Each person took his or her own property, which, before land ownership, involved personal property such as beads, clothing, and tools. Any children born to the couple usually remained with the mother.

Marriage among contemporary Ga'dang is markedly different than it was during the 1965–66 study. Marriage is based on courtship. Marriage can no longer be defined as an alliance between families, although subtle suggestions and pressure can be placed on a young man or a young woman to seek out the friendship of a particular person. It may be that two families would like their children to marry, but a go-between is no longer used in arranging a marriage. Child betrothal is no longer practiced. Marriage among the Ga'dang in Bananao, however, still takes place at a relatively young age: some girls are around 14 or 15 years of age and boys are around 17 to 20 years of age. This is especially the case when young Ga'dang drop out of high school. If the young men and women stay in school, marriage is deferred until the early 20s.

Marriage often comes about when the girl becomes pregnant. When this happens, the parents may get together and decide what each family is going to contribute to the couple to form a new household. This is a modern version of the practice of the past. If the young man does not want to marry the girl, his family can pay the girl's parents a fee—usually cash, pigs, or a carabao. There also have been cases where the young man merely moves away from the village and does not return until he hears that the girl has married. Both options for the young man existed in the past.

Young Ga'dang are proud that they have the freedom to chose their own mate without serious interference from their parents and are quick to point out they are now "civilized." Because Ga'dang villages are much larger than in the past, young people no longer are encouraged to look for a mate outside of their own village. Young people court one another, regardless of ethnic background, and ultimately marry.

There is no elaborate marriage ceremony, although the Family Code of the Philippines requires an officially married couple to be registered. Sometimes, after the couple goes to the Poblacion of Paracelis and is married by the municipal court, or after the couple is married by a Christian minister, a party may be held for the couple by the parents of the boy.

Divorce is not legally possible in the Philippines. Nevertheless, as in the past, people dissolve their marriage when they agree to separate. A separated person can start living with another person; while this union might be considered a marriage by the local people, it is not recognized as such by the Philippine government. Reasons for separation today are similar to the reasons given for the 1960s. At separation, the two parties take from the marriage what they brought to the marriage in the form of land or other possessions. If new land or other wealth has been acquired during the marriage, it is either divided or given to the children if they are older. As in the past, children usually stay with the mother.

During the restudy, I noticed that occasionally younger people would substitute Ilocano kinship terms for Ga'dang kin terms, or they might use the terms interchangeably. This prompted me to revisit basic Ga'dang kinship terminology, and after I had a list of people living in the community, I was able to ask in Ga'dang the question: "How are you related to X?" and "How are you related to Y?" In the 45-year-period between the two studies, Ga'dang kinship terminology, at least at one level of specification, did not change. Basic Ga'dang kin terms for 1965 and the present are, as follows:

ama: Father. Distinctive criteria: consanguineal; first ascending generation; lineal; male.

ina: Mother. Distinctive criteria: consanguineal; first ascending generation; lineal; female.

anak: Child. Distinctive criteria: consanguineal; first descending generation; lineal; male and female.

ulitag: Parents' brothers and male cousins; husbands of parents' sisters and female cousins. Distinctive criteria: consanguineal; first ascending generation; collateral; male.

ikit: Parents' sisters and female cousins; wives of parents' brothers and male cousins. Distinctive criteria: consanguineal; first ascending generation; collateral; female.

kolak: Siblings. Distinctive criteria: consanguineal; Ego's generation.

kapingsan: Cousins. Distinctive criteria: consanguineal; Ego's generation.

panganakan: Children of siblings and cousins; children of spouse's siblings and cousins. Distinctive criteria: consanguineal; first descending generation; collateral.

afu: Grandparents; ascendants of grandparents; siblings, cousins, and siblings' and cousins' spouses of grandparents; grandchildren; grandchildren of siblings and cousins and of their spouses' siblings and cousins; descendants of the foregoing. Distinctive criteria: consanguineal; more than one generation removed.

atawa: Spouse. Distinctive criteria: affinal; Ego's generation.

katawangan: Spouse's parents; spouse's parents' siblings and cousins and their spouses. Distinctive criteria: affinal; first ascending generation; lineal.

manuwang: Spouses of sons and daughters; spouses of siblings. Distinctive criteria: affinal; first ascending generation; lineal.

kafalay: Child's spouse's parents and their siblings, cousins, and the siblings' and cousins' spouses. Distinctive criteria: affinal; Ego's generation; lineal.

kabirat: Spouse's siblings' spouses. Distinctive criteria: affinal; Ego's generation; collateral.

During the restudy, I was unable to discern any changes in the basic kinship terminology system of the Ga'dang. What was clearly apparent, however, was a difference in the use of kin terms between people over 40 years of age and under 40 years of age. Impressionistically, older people use kin terms more often than younger people. Even older children know the kin terms associated with the immediate household, as well as grandparents, grandchildren, aunts and uncles, and immediate cousins. Few people, however, can articulate the more complicated concepts associated with bilateral kin groups and distant relatives. Immediate kin, mainly parents and children, siblings, and cousins, are still important to the Ga'dang, but kinship as an institution has lost much of its importance since the time of the earlier study. During the earlier study, both the kinship terms of reference (i.e., "How are you related to X?") and the vocative terms, although less so than terms of reference, were the everyday norm. Children would be corrected by adults if they should misuse a kin term. Today, Ilocano kin terms are used interchangeably with Ga'dang kin terms. Forty-five years ago, when head-hunting and danger was in the recent memory of the older Ga'dang, kin were perceived as paramount to, and almost synonymous with, safety. A Ga'dang wanted and needed as many real and fictive relatives as possible. This need is no longer given a high priority by the Ga'dang.

When a Marriage Is Not a Marriage

In 1965–66, the Ga'dang practiced a form of temporary marriage, which they called *solyad*, and I translated as "spouse exchange." Illicit sexual relations were common, but this type of activity was not recognized by the Ga'dang as spouse exchange. At the time, 40 percent of the adults had participated in a solyad. My first knowledge of the solyad came in 1966 after spending the night in Bayongyong. Walking toward Paracelis the next morning, I asked my Ga'dang companion why the male host of the house in which I slept was different from my male host when I got up in the morning. He looked at me, smiled, and said, "They had just completed a solyad."

Spouse exchange was a complicated and elaborate social negotiation, like marriage, between two families. Consider the following. The possibility of exchanging wives is discussed informally by two men—for purposes of illustration, Ita and Buwak. The men discuss the possibility with one another, and each man discusses the possibility with his wife. If all four people agree, the negotiations and formal arrangements are then made by the parents of one of the men.

For example, Ita would ask his parents to approach the parents of Buwak to negotiate the solyad. The parents of the women did not enter into the negotiations. The parents of Ita would visit the parents of Buwak, and after considerable insignificant small talk, Ita's parents would bring up the topic of the solyad. This comes as no surprise to Buwak's parents, as their son had already informed them of the forthcoming visit from Ita's parents. Ita's father would inform Buwak's parents that his son wants to solyad with their son and daughter-in-law. Buwak's father would say that he and his wife will consider the proposal.

A few days later, Ita's parents returned to the home of Buwak's parents, bringing with them a kiring, some betel nut, and wine. This meeting—called *maman* (betel nut chewing)—marked the beginning of the solyad negotiations. The parents of Ita would offer one kiring as collateral to the parents of Buwak as a symbol of good faith that Ita would follow culturally prescribed behavior during the solyad. The offer of one kiring would probably not be acceptable to Buwak's parents. The negotiation between the two families was fundamentally a social challenge, reflecting verbal but friendly conflict, with friendship as the ultimate goal of the negotiations. Consequently, Buwak's parents would put up one kiring as matching collateral and suggest another maman. In general, solyad negotiations took three maman and involved two kiring and one lufay (a bead earring of considerable value). The collateral was an integral part of the solyad because if either Ita or Buwak or their wife counterparts should break the rules of the solyad, the family's collateral would be forfeited (see Wallace 1969).

At the end of the third maman, Ita would go to the house of Buwak, and Buwak would go to the house of Ita. During the solyad, there were culturally prescribed forms of behavior for all four individuals, a special set of fictive kin terms were used, and provisions were made for children born from the solyad. The solyad usually lasted for six months to a year. After termination, the collateral was returned to the original owners, and the couples were free to enter into a new solyad if they so desired.

The solyad is no longer practiced by the Ga'dang. There are no vestiges of the practice, and when asked about the solyad, people responded with, "We are Christians now," or "It causes problems in marriage." Some of the younger Ga'dang have never heard of the practice of solyad. Forty-five years ago, the Ga'dang said that they entered into spouse exchange to demonstrate that they had *madaiyao* (an indefinable form of power similar to the type of power ascribed to men who had taken many heads), to conceive a child when a woman could not get pregnant with her husband, and most importantly, to expand the number of relatives—in this case fictive relatives. Lacking in broadly based sociopolitical unity in the past, the dispersed Ga'dang settlements were linked together through a formal and informal network of kin with their associated obligations. Like taking a spouse from a distant village, the solyad served to expand social ties and enhance safety. In the restudy of the Ga'dang, safety is the responsibility of the state.

Still Talking about Head-Hunting

Although it has been many years since the Ga'dang last took a head, very old men and women occasionally bring up the topic even if I am not querying them on the issue. From an interpretive perspective, these elderly men and woman still take pride in the culture that has been lost. It is not so much that they miss the past, as they live in a modern world, but for their generation, it is a part of what it is to be "Ga'dang."

Despite their reputation for head taking, to my knowledge, the last time the Ga'dang took a head was in 1965. During the 1965–66 study, I tried to gather information on recent head-taking practices, but the Ga'dang were reluctant to discuss the matter, mainly because they were still in active conflict with lowlanders encroaching on their traditional lands, and they were fearful of the constabulary. I would estimate, based on general conversations with men and women at the time, that somewhere between 50 and 70 percent of the men over the age of 50 had either taken one head or been on at least one head-taking raid. This means that the men would have been born around 1915, and in their late 20s during World War II, a period of renewed head-taking activities in the Cordillera Central. This is in contrast to the reports of the studies on the Ilongot, a tribal minority of the Cordillera Central located south and east of the Ga'dang (M. Rosaldo 1980; R Rosaldo 1980).

Michelle and Renato Rosaldo started researching the Ilongot three years after I started my study of the Ga'dang and report that in 1968 around 90 percent of the men over the age of 20 had taken at least one head. This suggests that Ilongot were more active for a longer period of time than other hill tribes in the area. The head-taking activities of the Ilongot appeared to have been monitored more closely by the Philippine press than the activities of other hill tribes, possibly because of the legacy associated with the three Ilongot who murdered the anthropologist William Jones discussed earlier. The first time I went into the Ilongot area in 1965, I had great difficulty recruiting lowlanders to accompany me because of the head-hunting reputation of the Ilongot. In fact, on the night before we were to arrive at an Ilongot village after poling up the Cagayan River to its headwaters, my lowland Ilocano companions disappeared during the night. As noted earlier, I had been warned numerous times about the dangers of going into Ga'dang territory, but I never had companions abandon me during the night on my way to the Ga'dang area.

I first learned about a recent head taking soon after I started living in the small Ga'dang village of Pakak in 1965. The following is taken directly from my journal:

Journal entry, Pakak, October 1965

At times like this, I fully realize my incompetence in speaking and understanding Gaddang. I have for the past hour been sitting in front of Bilongan's house listening to Nisit, Bilongan, Kabet, and Rogilo discuss two major topics: the recent murder of two Ilocano and the habits and activities of monkeys. It would have been inappropriate for me to interrupt the conversation for a translation. I knew about the murders as I was present in San Mateo when the funeral procession passed by. The San Mateo rumor is that the murderers are Ga'dang from Pakak. I don't believe the rumor. It is my impression that Bilongan, Nisit, and Kabet think the crime was committed by four Ga'dang from Laya, a community about three hours' walking from here. The pattern was kill, cut the neck [removing the head] and fingers, and burn the house. Although this pattern conforms to some degree with the beliefs of the Ga'dang, it does not mean that the killings were committed by Ga'dang.

Traditionally, the Ga'dang took heads to avenge a wrong, and to gain status. They seldom discriminated between men, women, and children, although the preference was status for status; for example, in a feud, a head taken from a high-status person should be countered with the head of a person of equally high status. More often than not, lone individuals were attacked by small groups of men who took the head; public battles were seldom undertaken. The practical aspects of dismembering a head from the body of a victim were relatively simple; the head taker pulls the hair of the deceased with one hand, places his foot on the deceased body, and then chops the neck with a head axe or a machete. I was told in the earlier study by a former headhunter that a strong man could sever the head from the body with two swift cuts. To avenge a wrong, or in a standing feud, the Ga'dang took heads from enemy Ga'dang villages and from other tribal groups. They also took the heads of lowlanders, and ultimately the Japanese, for perceived wrongs and during general hostilities.

Similar to their neighbors the Ifugao and the Kalinga, the Ga'dang sometimes would keep the heads in their houses as a tribute to their exploits (Barton 1938; Dozier 1967), but only if the head was from the Ga'dang or a member of another mountain tribe. It was a way to honor and respect their fallen enemies. The heads of Ilocano lowlanders and the Japanese were not kept. Instead, the heads were thrown away or buried to show the Ga'dang's contempt for them. A common and often stated belief among the Ga'dang of the 1965–66 study was that the Ilocano and the Japanese had no honor. The Ga'dang also cut off the tip of the deceased little finger, which often would be placed in a pot of food that was being cooked and then eaten. Later the finger bone could be strung as part of a man's necklace.

When the raiding party returned to the village with a head, there was a dance, an oratory recounting taking the head, with the audience expecting eloquence from the headhunters, and a celebration feast. The raiding party accrued status for their act. The man who led the raiding party and took the head was accorded the greatest status. A man who had led many expeditions attained the status of *mingal*. It was a way to show that the man had great madaiyao, the Ga'dang concept of indefinable "power" discussed earlier. Taking a head was not a requisite for getting a bride, a popular myth often told in the lowlands. Some Ga'dang may have contributed to this myth, however, as another way of keeping lowlanders from encroaching into their mountainous area. The successful head-hunting exploits of the family, nevertheless, afforded a young man better marriage opportunities.

The traditional Ga'dang practices and concepts associated with head-hunting (cf. Hoskins 1996) contained some features of head taking found among the Kalinga as described by Edward Dozier (1966), the Ifugao as described by Roy Barton (1938), and the Ilongot as described by Michelle Rosaldo (1980). The Kalinga brought the head back to the village, held a feast and dance, and placed the skull in a community sepulcher for future generations to see. The primary motivating factor was to gain status. The Ifugao sometimes brought not only the head but also the arms, legs, and hands of the slain enemy back to the village. The skull was kept in the house of the man who made the kill. Some Ifugao associated the taking of heads with a cure for sickness and as a necessity for the fertility of the rice. Although the Ilongot had a celebration after taking a head, they threw the head away. It was the act of killing, and according to Renato Rosaldo:

> To take a head is, in Ilongot terms, not to capture a trophy, but to "throw
> away" a body part, which by principle of sympathetic magic represents
> the cathartic throwing away of certain burdens of life—the grudge an
> insult has created, or the grief over a death in the family, or the increasing
> "weight" of remaining a novice when one's peers have left that status.
> (1980:140)

The Ga'dang had no Kalinga-like community resting place for enemy
heads, although they occasionally kept a skull in the house, especially if it
belonged to a high-status person. Otherwise, they discarded it, buried it, or
left it to rot. I have no evidence to suggest that taking a head for the Ga'dang
was in any way linked to anything like the Ilongot's concept of "throw away."
Perhaps taking a head could be related to sympathetic magic because the
Ga'dang occasionally attributed the curing of an illness to a successful head-
taking raid.

The People's Court

During the 1965–66 study, while peace and security were theoretically
the responsibility of the Philippine government, in reality, the Ga'dang, as did
many of the hill peoples, established their own peace pact system, called in
Ga'dang a *pudon*. The Ga'dang pudon operated much like the peace pact system of the Kalinga (Barton 1949; Dozier 1966), except it was not as elaborate. The Ga'dang of Pakak and Cabanuangan had a pudon with several
settlements located in the mountains to the west, some with other Ga'dang
villages, and with Ifugao and Balangao speakers. Establishing a pudon,
which included participation in the exchange of gifts and food and in oratory
and dancing, meant the members of the communities could travel in one
another's territory without fear of harm. If an event such as a theft or murder
occurred, the leaders of the peace pact would get together and reach an agreement as to what type of reprisal would be taken. The punishment was a fine,
with the fine depending on the crime. The peace pact operated only within
the territories of the pudon villages. In addition to helping maintain peace
and order, the pudon also had strong economic implications. The communities of Pakak and Cabanuangan were particularly in demand as peace pact
partners because they were located within a one-day walk to the lowland
towns in Isabela where many of villagers took their mountain products to
trade or sell. The peace pact provided people from the higher mountains a
place to sleep on their way to the lowlands.

The peace pact system no longer operates among the Mountain Ga'dang.
There is, however, a local People's Court or Dispute-Mediator Council (*Lupong
Tagapamayapa* or written as *Lupon* in Bananao). This is a common barangay
practice in the rural Philippines. There is considerable regional variation in dispute interpretation and resolution, especially with regard to punishment.

In Bananao, for example, the people's court is reminiscent of the pudon system in that it is presided over by the people, both sides of a dispute are represented, and punishment is levied by the council. In Bananao, the court consists of eight people who are appointed by the Elected Barangay Council, and it reflects the ethnic diversity of the community. The members are selected for the court because they are respected and trusted members of the community, which means they are usually elderly and male, although women do serve on the court. This court deals with locally disruptive issues such as slander, stealing, harassment, fighting, public drunkenness, and shouting too much in public. More egregious behavior such as chronic theft by a person, armed robbery, or murder falls under the jurisdiction of the municipal police and courts. The court meets when a complainant files a case against another party, which is usually only once or twice a month. The two parties appear before the court, present their arguments, and the court decides on guilt or innocence and levies a fine. The philosophy of the court is to punish wrongdoers with a heavy fine and/or try to resolve conflicts between parties so that there is peace in the community. There is no official language of the Lupon, but the languages used in the court are Ilocano, maybe some Ga'dang and Balangao, a little English, and perhaps a Tagalog word or two. One example will serve to illustrate.

A member of the Lupon in Bananao received the following notification (names used here are fictitious):

> OFFICE OF THE LUPON TAGAPAMAYAPA
> July-10-2010
> To: June Kakaret
> Dear June,
> Pakaamo kadakyo amin nga Lupon adda ti kaso tayo
> no bigat ti agasopa, June 11, ano 8:00 o'clock a.m. jay
> barangay hall.
> Anita Buget—complainant
> Maria Molino—respondent
> Darum na: moral defamation, grave threat
> Pica J. Gumilab
> Lupon Chairman

Anita Buget claimed that Maria Molino threatened her with a machete and chased her around the village. She wanted to be compensated for her suffering. Maria Molino claimed that she did this because Anita Buget was sleeping with her husband, so she was justified in chasing her. Maria claimed Anita had injured her by sleeping with her husband. Anita denied she was sleeping with Maria's husband.

The Lupon spent most of the afternoon discussing this case. The court decided that there was not enough evidence to judge Anita guilty of sleeping with Maria's husband. The evidence presented by both parties was too conflicting for the Lupon to support clearly either position. They felt this was more of a domestic issue than a Lupon issue. They, however, did decide that

Maria was guilty of slandering Anita and potentially causing her bodily harm. The punishment for Maria was to kill one pig for the wrong she had caused Anita. But, because the evidence of whether Anita was sleeping with Maria's husband was unclear, the pig had to be eaten by both families at the same time. In the view of the Lupon, the wrong of slander was rendered right by having Maria kill a pig. The disruptive nature of whether Anita was sleeping with Maria's husband—a community issue rather than a moral issue—was righted by forcing the two families to eat the pig together. This is a modern interpretation of traditional Cordillera Central tribal justice (see Barton 1919), and the Lupon serves the same social function as community justice did a hundred years ago.

Most of the dispute cases that come before the Lupon are far more mundane than the case of Anita and Maria. More typical would be settling a dispute between two families over where a fence should be placed, or one family complaining that their neighbor has too many pigs tied in the yard.

In Their Own Words

A culture is a composite set of common beliefs expressed and interpreted by individuals with common and unique life experiences. Life histories do not define culture, but they help to characterize culture. Even with the critical thinking associated with some of the epistemological, methodological, and interpretive issues of life history research (Linde 1993; Ochs and Capps 1996; Peacock and Holland 1993; Wallace 1987), life history remains an important part of ethnographic research. The histories are illustrative of life experiences in a culture. Moreover, life history data, or personal narratives, have been a part of the arsenal of ethnographic methods for many years, as clearly illustrated by Paul Radin's pioneering autobiography of a Winnebago Indian (1920), and more pertinent here, Roy Barton's research in the early 1900s leading to the autobiography of three Ifugao women (1938).

Four abbreviated or condensed life histories are included here, one of an elderly woman, one of an elderly man, one of a middle-aged woman, and one of a younger woman. In collecting the narratives, I endeavored to ask open-ended questions that would encourage the person randomly to remember important events in his or her life, while concurrently guiding the narrative toward a coherent order. In critiquing this approach, I am responsible for adding some order where there may have been none. The data were gathered speaking Ga'dang, Ilocano, and English. After translation into English, I made no attempt to correct grammatical structure. These narratives are presented as a mechanism to introduce the reader to the humanity of four Ga'dang and bring life to the subjects of the study. They are neither typical nor atypical of life for a Ga'dang, but they do reflect what it means to be Ga'dang. The condensed narratives that follow are from real people, only their names are fictional.

APRING, FEMALE, AGE 85?
Bayongyong, 2010

I'm a very old woman. I don't know my age . . . maybe I'm 87 or 86. I was born in Paracelis before it was a place. My daughter says I was born in 1920 or 1925. We had no need to know our age. I don't know. My village was Bakari. It was a big village . . . maybe more than 15 or 20 houses. I don't remember.

Maybe I was 12 when I was first married. His name was Tolai, and we moved to his village before my first daughter was born. He was many years older. I think 30 years older than me. He died after my last daughter was born. I don't know what year. My parents had me marry him because he was willing to give a kiring for me and some pigs, and some rice cakes, and a three-day celebration for me. It was a big celebration with many visitors. After one year I had Dangao . . . she is here with me now. You know her . . . she is my blind daughter living here. You know her. She's also old.

Two years later I had my second child, a girl. Then in two more years I had my third girl. In another year I had a different girl, and then in four years I had my last daughter. I never had any boys. All of my daughters live here in Bayongyong.

After my husband died I didn't have a husband, but it was no problem. In a few years I got a second husband, but I didn't have any more children. He died maybe 30 years ago. I never got another husband.

I can't remember all the changes that have happened in my life. So much. Everything is changed . . . it is very different. One thing that is very good from when I was a small child is we now have matches. When I was a kid we used a flint to start a fire or we had to rub bamboos together to start a fire. We always had to be careful that we keep the fire burning in the hearth. If it went out, we had to start it again. It is easier now.

I remember my father and my mother, but I remember my father the best. He was a great and powerful Ga'dang warrior. He had much more madaiyao. He had more than other men. He was already a great warrior before the Japanese came, but when the Japanese came, he became even a greater warrior. He took many Japanese heads . . . as many as any Ga'dang. When I was a child and a young woman I remember many ceremonies when the men came back to the village with heads. The ceremonies were great celebrations. We honored all Ga'dang, Ifugao, and Kalinga whose heads the men brought back with ceremonies and dances. The dance would last all night. The men also cut off the fingers of the Ga'dang they killed and the fingers of the other men from other hill tribes. It gave them madaiyao. Later the bones would be made into necklaces for the men. After the heads decayed, the skulls were hung in the house. They also made stoppers for betel nut lime holders out of the fingers.

During World War II we had to run away because the Japanese were strong here. Some Ga'dang went north and west high into the mountains. Other Ga'dang found safety with relatives in other forests. The Japanese were very cruel. Your friend Sollay escaped to Natonin. We all saw the Japanese tie his grandfather's arms behind his back and throw him in the river. He drowned. That is why we wanted to cut off the heads of the Japanese. The heads were thrown away. The Japanese had no honor.

The Japanese and the Ilocano were not worth honoring. They had no madaiyao.

Head taking ended after the war.

DOMIGAN, MALE, AGE 96?
Bayongyong, 2010

I was born in Banagao in Aurora a long time ago. When some of us registered in Paracelis after World War II, I was told I was born in 1914. I'm the oldest Ga'dang here in Bananao . . . maybe anywhere. There is one woman here around my age. Maybe I am older than her. Maybe she is older than me. We are both old.

I'm the only one here that remembers when we Ga'dang were fighting all the time and we took many heads. It was a bad time when I was just a boy. There was always danger. We always worried about being attacked. No one was safe . . . man or woman. The Ilocano were after our land we had to defend ourselves. There were many of them coming in from the lowlands. They wanted our forest to make uma on. Also the Balangao wanted our land. I never have to worry too much now. Life is more peaceful.

I never had the honor of taking a head, but I was always there when we had the celebration. That honor of taking the head was reserved for the older men who led us. Before the war, I went on three trips where heads were taken. The first one was when I was a very young man. The man we killed was a Ga'dang who had wronged our family. He was an enemy who had broken into my grandfather's granary and stolen some things. We had to avenge the family. Two other times I went with other men to kill an Ilocano. They were trying to steal Ga'dang land. My father went to prison for eight years.

The greatest Ga'dang to ever take heads was Lamisan . . . he took over ten heads, maybe more. Mainly he took Ilocano heads, but also some Ga'dang enemy heads. We treated the heads differently. The Ilocano did not deserve being placed on a pole. They did not deserve the honor. We put their heads on rice pestle so we could have an anitu and dance around it. Later put in a pot and eat. We would get their madaiyao when we ate their fingers. We don't want to eat Ilocano. Lamisan had the greatest madaiyao because he had so many heads.

Finally after the war, the forests were going away, and there were too many Ilocano accusing us of things so I moved to Butigue. I was around 35 then. I never married until I moved to Butigue across the river. I married Bukaku. They named her Bukaku because she had so many head lice when she was a baby. She was seven years old when we were married. She was from Butigue. I gave her parents the kiring and some pigs. I took care of her until after she started menstruating. That is when we started having sex. We had five boys and one girl. She died giving birth to the seventh child. This was in the time of Marcos when she died. I was already in my 60s by then. My sons wanted me to make sure I could get the land that was open to the Ga'dang. They said more children would mess things up. So I did not get a new wife.

TANGIN, FEMALE, AGE 46
Bayongyong, 2010

I was born on the west side of the Magat River . . . in the municipality of San Mateo or Potia I don't know which municipality . . . I don't know . . . in 1964. The closest Ga'dang village was Pakak. I had one older brother and one older sister. They were also born where I was born. I don't remember the place, but I know it was a small village with less than ten houses. We were very poor. We only had one small uma. That's what we did then.

When I was around five we moved with my father and my older brother and sister to Kaipilan. Kaipilan was bigger. Fifteen or 20 houses. My father's name was Baladong. The forest was disappeared in the San Mateo area and the Ilocano were taking our land. We had many disagreements with the Ilocano . . . they always wanted our land. In those days we could not live with the Ilocano, but today it is different. Now there is no forest for anybody.

When I was around nine years old, we moved to Ngileb. Now Ngileb is in Potia or Alfonso Lista. When we moved to Ngileb there was still forest to farm. No more today. It is all gone. No uma now. Everybody now farms with the plow. It was in Ngileb where my mother dies. She died of a very large and swollen stomach [*lulud*].

We left Ngileb for Bananao looking for a better place to live. Life was hard in Ngileb. Our uma did not produce enough rice for my father, and us children. I remember being hungry. We came here when I was around 12. We moved here to Bayongyong because there was still some forest then for our uma. We had a big uma then. Now our uma is far into the mountains. We have very far to go.

I got married here in Bayongyong at age 14. Our marriage was arranged. I didn't want but what could I do? I was not happy. I cried. The *walang* [gifts of one kiring, one pig, and some money] had already been given to my father and his new wife. I had no choice. I had to marry him. My father sold the kiring a long time ago to a woman in Baguio.

After I got married, my life was to have children and work with my husband in the uma.

My first child was born in 1980. She was born with epilepsy so she still lives with me. She never marry. The men no want her here because of the expense of her medicine. But she understands. Her name is Lingtu. We did not give her a Ga'dang name. We are Christians. I sometimes worry. You never know when she will have an attack. Sometimes often, and sometime maybe just once a month. You never know. She cannot eat any kinds of fat . . . especially pork fat because it gives her an attack. Sometimes she had problems thinking. She could not go to school. She is a good help in the house and helping in the uma.

My second daughter was born year after my first daughter in 1981. She was born like any other baby. She attended elementary school and can speak English. She is now working in Dubai as a domestic. She does not like living in Dubai. The people treat her badly. The men always expect her to have sex with them. She wants to come home but she has a contract. She cannot leave. Her salary is good, and sometimes she can send money home to us. Unfortunately, much of the money she gets goes to the company that arrange for her to get the job. Their charge is almost half of what she receives in Dubai.

It is very odd that I did not want to marry my husband. In total, I had 11 children . . . six girls and five boys. I had four children die at birth. They were all born in my house with the help of the mafuyat.

JULE, FEMALE, AGE 29
Bayongyong, 2010

My official registered name when I was born is Jule Madonyao. My father gave me the name of Jule. I was born here in Bananao in 1981. My mother was Ricka. She was from Bagabag, which is a remote barangay of Paracelis. My father married her when she was around 17 and he was around 30.

My mother had my older sister a year after my father married her. According to my father, this marriage was arranged between his parents and her parents. I don't know how. My father didn't have any kiring or anything to give my mother's parents. I guess his mother and father gave them something. When I was one or two years of age my mother took me to Bagabag and I lived there until I was eight years old. I was so very happy the day my father came and got me, and brought me back to Bananao. I was eight. I was very unhappy in Bagabag.

My father and my mother could not be happy together. I didn't get to go to elementary when I was living with my mother. That's why I was late starting to school. I didn't start elementary until I came here to live with my father. I graduated elementary. Then I went to high school in Butigue. It was a four kilometer walk each day. But I graduated. I wanted to go to college but we had not money.

My mother got a new husband when I was little. My father did not get a new wife. She left him because he was going blind and he could not support her. My father was your good friend. You saw how he was going blind. I tried to take care of him.

I only saw my sister one time since I was a little girl. That was when she came here when my father died. I was happy she came to see him at death.

I was 24 years old when I got married. That was very old for a Ga'dang, but I wanted to go to school. My husband is from Natonin, but he has relatives here. I met him here in Bananao. He courted me for three years before we were married. I had my first child the first year I was married. We could not afford to have a minister marry us. It was too expensive We could not afford to kill pigs; invite relatives, clothes and more. We went to the Poblacion and the Mayor married us. It was free. We decided to live here because I have a little land my father left to me.

My land is very small, only one-forth hectare. I inherited it from my father. He told me he bought the land a long time ago.

At first we grew corn on the land, but for only one-forth hectare it was too expensive to grow corn. It is very costly for plowing, weed killer, fertilizer, bug spray, and the thrashing. We decided we would be better off to grow upland rice and vegetables on our little piece of land. But last year we harvested 30 bundles of rice, but it is not enough for the whole year. We need at least one tarot each day for my husband, three children, and me. We also grow bananas, squash, eggplant, and chili.

Since my husband is from Natonin we speak Ga'dang, Balangao, and Ilocano in the house.

When my father died we only waited four days to bury him because we had no money. We could not afford a funeral. I feel very guilty that I could not buy him his medicine. He had TB. He died early in the morning so I immediately called my neighbors to help me. I didn't know what to do; the neighbors dressed my father in some clothes you had given him on your last visit. They were his best clothes. But he had no shoes. I wanted him to look good. A man from the village came and injected him with formaldehyde to preserve him. It cost 600 pesos. A neighbor was good to me and paid the man. We could not afford to feed the visitors, so there was no ceremony. The neighbors built a *darara* shed for the visitors to sit in. His body was placed in the house. After he was dressed, he was placed on a bench so visitors could come to look at him.

Three of his old friend and some neighbors dug a grave for my father. He wanted to be buried by his house but the road had cut much of the land away. It was hard to dig because a cave had to be cut into the side of the sloping land so he would not wash away. After he was put in the ground, rocks were place over the opening to the cave.

Extra clothes, and food and water were placed in the grave so he would have plenty in the afterlife. I put his walking stick on top of his grave.

Ever year on the day of his death, I give him a little food and water for his journey. I wish I had more to give him.

Chapter 6

Getting Right with God

Spiritual Change

*O*ratorical challenges during certain rituals were an important feature of traditional Ga'dang culture. During the ritual, a man, usually old, would stand up and challenge other men to recount their exploits in taking heads, killing crocodiles, killing snakes, or surviving attacks from enemies. This was done in a chanting, sing-song-speaking style, emphasizing the exploits of the man and his family, either past or present, with an orientation toward what might be called bragging with humility. Late one night in 1966, the following brief introduction to a challenge oratory was recorded by me at a ritual designed to exorcize an evil spirit that had possessed a man. The translation is as close to the original Ga'dang as possible.

> Put down your gong three
> gather and listen my friends.
> I challenge you to listen carefully
> for what I am to do.
> For the sake of holding the cup
> because we are many
> who are gathered here to anitu.
> Let us fill our cups.
> It is hard to be proud but I tell you. . . .

After this introduction, the men then drank their sugarcane wine, and the speaker proceeded to recount how his father had been a great headhunter. This oratorical challenge was followed by another man's, and then another's.

Such oratorical challenges, and numerous other traditional rituals and spiritual beliefs, are no longer a part of Ga'dang culture. In this chapter, I compare the practices denoting ritual and religious life among the Ga'dang in 1965–66 with their practices and religious life in the present in an effort to

91

develop an explanatory model of change in a people's spiritual life. As will become apparent, measuring concepts associated with worldview, religious philosophy, and rituals is generally more complex than measuring changes associated with the environment, economy, and social organization.

Worldview and the Origin of Earth: 1965–66

In the 1965–66 study, the Ga'dang defined the total world of the past and the present as *ilosa*. Ilosa was divided into two realms; the "earth world" (*dufafa*) and the "up-after world" (*kalekay*). In Ga'dang mythology, ilosa was the place described as the point of origin of all living things, and the place where the important benevolent deity and culture hero, Nanolay (see appendix A), performed his noble deeds. In the original 1965–66 study, the Ga'dang said little about kalekay because it was a world about which they had only heard. They were more concerned with the dufafa because it was a place of famine, sickness, death, and uncertainty. It was the world of the immediate. It was the world in which they faced problems on a daily basis.

The hesitancy of the Ga'dang to discuss the up-after world did not grow out of fear of the unknown but out of a feeling of "not knowing." The most common response to a query about the up-after world was, "I don't know." Even very knowledgeable mediums responded with this answer. The typical response to a question about the up-after life was, "Nanolay, Ofag, and *kararawa.*"

The Ga'dang myth, "The Origin and the World and The Quarrel between Nanolay and Ofag" presented in appendix A illustrates some important features of traditional Ga'dang culture and helps define Nanolay and Ofag, and their relationship, especially as compared to the Ga'dang of the restudy. Ofag, the cousin of Nanolay, is in essence the antagonist of Nanolay. While he does not possess the powers of Nanolay, he nonetheless figures prominently in Ga'dang mythology and frequently creates situations that have to be countered by Nanolay.

For the Ga'dang of the 1960s, Nanolay was a cultural hero, a benevolent deity, responsible for the rats creating the earth as known by the Ga'dang. It should be noted, however, that Nanolay was not evoked or addressed directly by the Ga'dang, in common usage or in rituals. For example, it was improper to say in Ga'dang, "I beg (pray) to Nanolay"; such a statement would have been viewed by the Ga'dang as improper, even nonsensical. The myth clearly demonstrates important Ga'dang cultural concepts that are associated with why the world of the Ga'dang is as it is, why some animals and people are killed, how a right can adjust a wrong, the value of a go-between in negotiations, and the importance of beads. Whether Nanolay taking a bone (not necessarily a rib) from the sleeping man he created and then a woman appearing when he awoke is due to European influence remains unclear. In the myth, the type of bone from which the woman metamorphosed is not specified.

In addition, the myth provides insight into the dichotomy between the earth world and the up-after world, inhabited by *kararawa*, which may be translated as the "soul of a dead creature." In the Ga'dang universe of my original study, all creatures possessed a soul. For example, in Ga'dang, a person could say "the soul of a man," or the "soul of a pig," and it was a meaningful statement. At death, the souls of all creatures went to kalekay. There were two exceptions; a wild cat was reincarnated into an ant, and a chicken was reincarnated into a butterfly. I never found a Ga'dang who could explain these two exceptions to me.

Once in kalekay, the souls went about living the same life they had lived in the earth world. People argued, people killed, people made an uma, and humans and animals competed for limited resources. Kalekay, for the Ga'dang, was not considered a place of "heaven" as described in Christianity. It was not a place of reward for living a good life. It was simply a part of the life of all creatures, both animals and people. It was a common fate shared by all, both good and bad. Death was a normal part of life. The Ga'dang were far more oriented toward the dufafa, the earth world of here and now.

Because death was considered an inevitable part of life, while there were certain cultural prescriptions and proscriptions associated with death, burial was not a particular, spiritual event involving an elaborate funeral. As soon as a person died, he or she was moved to a small house constructed by neighbors and located very near the household. The house, called a *baowi* in Ga'dang, was small, without walls, and constructed on stilts. The deceased lay in the small house for three to five days while neighbors made a coffin from bamboo or planked wood. The husband or wife remained near the death house until the body was removed from the house and placed in the coffin. The body was dressed in a regular G-string if male or woven skirt if female. The only item of adornment was one string of beads for either a man or a woman.

A grave about six feet deep and wide enough for the casket was dug by male neighbors of the deceased. A somber funeral would take place early in the morning. Friends and relatives gathered at the grave site, but there were no prayers or rituals associated with the burial. One old man stood by and clapped two pieces of dry bamboo together as loudly as possible as a means of driving the spirits away. To help in making sure the deceased had daily comforts after death, those who wanted to participate placed offerings, such as a basket of rice, a plate, a bowl of water, and a betel nut bag with full paraphernalia, on the grave. Sharpened spikes of bamboo were frequently placed around the grave to drive away malevolent spirits.

The spouse of the deceased did not attend the funeral but instead moved to an empty house and mourned for five months. A man or woman would cover his or her head with a piece of cloth for this five-month period. After the five months, the spouse would remove the headscarf, throw away his or her clothing, and resume regular daily activities. If male, the person would now be addressed as *pangit* (widower) and, if female, as *balu* (widow). They

A typical grave in 1965 (*left*), and one in 2011.

would carry these terms of respect until they remarried, or if male, until he cut his hair.

Another concept that helped define the Ga'dang worldview was that of unting. Unting was a complex and interrelated set of beliefs associated with spiritually endowed objects. For example, when a family built a new house, before they could live in it, six unting were placed in the house, and an *agawa* ritual was held (discussed later). A house was not considered a Ga'dang home without the unting. The house unting hung from the rafters of the house, protected the house and its occupants from illness and other misfortune, and imposed the taboos of not eating corn or mudfish inside the house. The most revered and spiritually powerful of the unting was the *kubang*, on which the other five were dependent. It consisted of a bundle of clothing, generally a G-string, a skirt, and some beads, all of which had belonged to the parents or grandparents of the head of the household. The second most important piece was the *antolay*. This was a two-foot, round wooden pole, with the head of a man carved at one end. The other four house unting were the *alat* (a rattan ball with a chicken feather in it), the *buririraw* (a small bamboo fan), the *lutong* (a small piece of wood wrapped in rattan), and the *kuliwag* (the core of a piece of bamboo attached to a string of rattan).

In 1965–66, in response to the query, "What are the parts or characteristics of the earth world?" the common responses were "man, domesticated plants, ghouls, sickness—*amin* [all]." The Ga'dang at the time were particularly concerned with what they considered issues of physical danger from outsiders, and sickness. This preoccupation with danger should be seen in light of what was happening in area of the Ga'dang during the 1960s. It had been only 20 years since they had fled from the autocracies of the Japanese soldiers. Even the young people of the 1960s vividly and with fear remembered this period. Although head taking had been brought under control by the Philippine constabulary by then, the fears (and joys) associated with head taking were still topics of considerable discussion, especially among old men and women. This was also a period of extreme pressure on the Ga'dang because of the expanding number of Ilocano and other ethnic groups competing for the traditional forests of the Ga'dang, which were already being depleted. Finally, it was a time in the Philippines of a proliferation of governmental initiatives, especially from government agencies associated with family law, agrarian reform, and health. While these initiatives may have had a positive effect for most Filipinos, for a geographically isolated minority like the Ga'dang, these initiatives were simply additional pressures contributing to the uncertainty of life.

Sickness and Health: 1965–66

The Ga'dang have two basic classes of illness, "sickness," and "hurt." For example, if a person has what in English is called a "headache," in Ga'dang it would be described as a "sickness of the heads." What in Western medicine might be labeled tuberculosis, in Ga'dang would call a "sickness of spitting blood." The Ga'dang considered broken bones, muscle sprains, insect bites, and accidents as "hurts." In addition to the two classes of illness, the Ga'dang also identify some specific illnesses, the most common of which are blindness, insanity, birth defects, skin diseases, goiter, deafness, and malaria. They are so common they have a specific label, but as a group, they are considered sicknesses. Hurts are attributed mainly to natural causes. For example, an insect biting a person is "natural," just as a person cutting his or her hand with a knife is natural. Importantly, however, if, for example, a man is walking through the forest, and a limb falls on his head and he is injured, this might be attributed to a malevolent spirit that lives in the forest.

In 1965–66, malevolent spirits were a source of a great deal of uncertainty in the earth world and were responsible for most famine, sickness, general misfortune, and death. There were many malevolent spirits in the Ga'dang world in the earlier study. They all were equally dangerous to humans and served as an explanation for certain illnesses and deaths. The most common are described below.

The most frequently discussed malevolent spirits were *bingil*—physically distorted human-like ghouls that lived in the forest. They had very large eyes that reflected moonlight, and sometimes they seemed to glow in the dark. If a person should be so unfortunate as to encounter a bingil, the person would likely have a convulsion and die within two days.

The *aran* was a spirit creature that appeared in the form of a mist, often floating about the forest. This vapor-like creature had the ability to enter a human body. The most common attack method of the aran was to float into the village at night and take possession of a person's body while he or she was sleeping. When this happened, the person would begin to act erratically, go insane, and finally die.

The *angakokang* was an invisible creature known only from the sound it made in the most still part of the night. The sound was that of a whining or whimpering dog. It generally was not responsible for death, but hearing its whimper could cause illness.

Like bingil, *aled* were one of the most frequently discussed spirits of the Ga'dang. Aled were transubstantial spirits who, in their natural form, were invisible but had the power to change themselves into human and nonhuman forms. It was not uncommon for one of these spirits to disguise itself as a pig, a bird, or even a human. In their natural state, they lived in trees, rocks, stumps, and other objects in the forest. People had to be careful when walking alone in the forest because if an aled should reach out and touch a person, and aled were known to be aggressive, the person would immediately become dizzy, weak, and usually die within a few days. Aled were particularly dangerous because they occasionally had to kill someone—their main source of food was a human corpse.

All spirits were dangerous for the Ga'dang, but one of the most feared was a *karangat* (see appendix B). Like aled, they could transform themselves into any shape, but they were even more tricky and aggressive than aled. The karangat was sometimes visible and sometimes invisible. Its most distinctive characteristic was its long and sharp cusped teeth. It would lurk around the village in the form of a chicken or a post so it could not be recognized and reach out and touch people as they walked through the village. This would bring on sickness, insanity, and death. The only known means of killing a karangat was to trick it into letting a person stuff its mouth, eyes, and nose with betel nut, chewing leaves, and lime and then make sure that the lime was activated with water so then it would boil and chock the spirit to death.

In addition to the malevolent spirits that gave uncertainly to life, the Ga'dang also had to deal with many omens and taboos. One example will suffice as illustration. During the 1965–66 study, I had been on a long hiking trip with several Ga'dang companions. We had walked the whole day and were within one hour of our destination, but we still had at least two hours of daylight remaining. We had stopped to rest in the household of one of my companions, and just as we picked up our bags to leave, a child sneezed and a house lizard chirped. Both were omens of serious misfortune. One omen was bad enough; two omens at the same time were a disastrous sign. In my view, my companions showed sincere fear. We spent the night with the family and proceeded on our trip the next morning.

Since most "sicknesses" and "hurts" were caused by malevolent spirits, or because a person broke a taboo or disregarded an omen, the way to avoid death or prolonged illness was to turn to a Ga'dang ritual specialist. Mediums, both male and female, were usually elderly, and addressed with terms of respect meaning "old man" or "old woman." As previously mentioned, a male medium was a mabayen and female medium was a makamong. While there were both male and female mediums, the consensus was that women mediums had greater powers of divination and were more able to act as go-betweens in the spiritual world (Wallace 1975). Male mediums specialized in recounting myths and in singing and chanting ritual songs.

Mediums among the Ga'dang, like those in most other hill groups of the Cordillera Central, were part-time specialists (cf. Barton 1946, 1949, Cole

1915, Dozier 1966). They had the same economic and social responsibilities as any other member of society. Because of their special capabilities, however, they had an elevated status in Ga'dang society. They were rewarded well for their services and were on demand throughout much of the year. For the Ga'dang, rituals were primarily performed for the individual or the family. The recipients of the benefits of the ritual were as much onlookers as participants. Consequently, the mediums were needed at birth, when a child was named, at marriage, at funerals, and to generally help individuals and households cure illness and prevent misfortune. Mediums, especially women, served as effective go-betweens for humans and the spirits and deities that wandered between the kalekay and dufafa of the ilosa.

Ritualism: 1965–66

Almost all Ga'dang rituals served to insure a secure and good life while living on the earth. They represented an attempt on the part of humanity either to prevent or to cure misfortune. In Pakak and Cabanuangan in the 1960s, rituals were divided into two classes: anitu rites and other rites. The other rites were those primarily associated with purification and were designed to prevent misfortune and sickness, as well as to cure sickness and hurts.

In Ga'dang, anitu did not refer to ancestral spirits or a particular ceremony, as was often the case with other peoples in the Cordillera Central (see Barton 1946; Dozier 1966; Jenks 1905). The most succinct statement on anitu by a Ga'dang in 1965 was "anitu is the thing (one, belief) followed by all men." For the Ga'dang, anitu was not a deity, a single ceremony, or a spirit; it was a belief in a spiritual power. Anitu had two basic usages. In the first usage, anitu was a power, force, or concept through which the important benevolent deity, Nanolay, is addressed. As noted, it would be incorrect in Ga'dang to say, "I beg to Nanolay." The correct utterance would be "I beg to anitu." For example, a medium, when calling on the spirit world to help in curing an illness, would say, *"kalakanak se ma'ari penad yo bunadu"* (please help me remove this one sickness). In the second usage, anitu represented seven rituals through which all Ga'dang participate before death.

Ga'dang anitu rituals were held to insure a harmonious relationship

Praying at a household rite, 1965.

between all Ga'dang, spaced over a period of a lifetime, and the spiritual world in order to moderate the uncertainties in life. The anitu rituals also served as a means for families to attain social status, and functioned to promote social occasions where large numbers of people gathered for good conversation, drinking, eating, dancing, and general gaiety. The seven anitu rituals of the Ga'dang of my 1965–66 study are briefly described, as follows:

- *agagwa*. Every time a Ga'dang family constructed a new house, it needed to be ritually purified to insure that no malevolent spirits could enter the house. This was usually a relatively short ritual, three or four hours, officiated by two female mediums, and involved the sacrifice of only one chicken. The participants were mainly from the immediate village. While culturally important, it was not an elaborate affair.

- *kurawit*. This was the first anitu sponsored by a newly formed household, usually held during the first year of marriage, but often in the second year of marriage because it required amassing large amounts of surplus food and drink. The event would be announced a month or so before it was to be held to insure large numbers of people would attend; the more people who attended, the more successful the social event. Ritual success was guaranteed simply by holding the anitu. Enough food and wine would be accumulated to render at least a full night of social dancing. One or more pigs would be killed. The kurawit required the service of one female medium, maybe two, and one male medium. This anitu was first a ritual in support of a safe and prosperous family life, but it was also a social and status-defining occasion. The hope of the household members and their families was that the kurawit would be discussed by other Ga'dang for many months to come.

- *balog*. This child's anitu was held for either a boy or a girl around the age of nine or ten. Occasionally, a household would hold the balog for two children at the same time. Having the event for two children, however, did not carry as much prestige as holding the rite separately for each child. Holding this ritual required planning and the gathering of large amounts of food and wine, and the killing of one or more pigs. The ritual validated important spiritual and social functions, and it differed from other anitu in that toward the end of the ceremony, the child becomes an active participant in the celebrations. There was a special dance for boys and for girls. Just before the special dance, one of the mediums killed a chicken and placed the blood on the forehead of the child. This baptism of blood was an overt symbol that the child was now a full member in the world of humanity and the spirits.

- *makadwa* and *maka'lu*. These two anitu were two of the most important spiritual and social events for the Ga'dang. Structurally, these anitu are the same, except that they are held at different times in the life of a household head, usually in the late 20s for the makadwa and in the late 30s for the maka'lu. By the time of these two anitu, the household head and his wife should be able to demonstrate economic success (with triumph in head-hunting in the distant past) by having on hand a surplus of rice, wine, and at least three pigs for sacrifice. These celebrations of life and success marked that the household was reaching the status of *kamaran* or "wealthy family." By this time in life, a man and woman should have greatly expanded their circle of fictive kin and friends, so many people would be expected to attend the affair. Like most Ga'dang rituals of the time, spiritual activities were the responsibility of the mediums. The members of the household hosted the event and enjoyed the joviality of the activities.

- *among*. The among was the most important of the anitu rites. Although not the last anitu for a household, it was the social high point of the household. All Ga'dang aspired to reach this level of social status, but few ever did. It was the most expensive of the anitu, requiring the most careful of planning and greatest accumulation of food, wine, and sacrificial pigs.

The among differs from other anitu because it was held with a partner, usually a cousin, but the partner could be a nonrelative. The partner was called a *tuwan*. The man of the household sponsoring the among would serve as the *tuwan* of his partner at another time. It was a great honor to be selected as a tuwan. The tuwan furnished some rice and one pig for the among. In addition, he provided a center pole (*arawarawi*) for dancing, a pair of lufay (already described), and a small wood-carved bird.

Like the other anitu, the among was primarily social, with mediums assuming the responsibility for performing the ritual. It was a time when boys met girls, and people made arrangements to visit one another; they planned hunting trips, played games, held oratory contests, and generally participated in a joyous occasion.

- *binatung*. This was the last of the anitu. It had great spiritual significance, but it marked the end of the anitu and carried little social importance. It was a small local affair, officiated by two mediums, and involved sacrificing only one pig. A family's social status had already been established by the time of the binatung.

To illustrate a Ga'dang ritual, one that is neither elaborate nor simple, but is representational, I present a description of a balog for a brother and sister, ages ten and 12 respectively, taken directly from my notes from January 1966. The family has accumulated one medium-sized pig, one cavan of rice (50 kilograms in 1966), and five cases of Black Hawk gin (a cheap commercial Philippine gin) for the event. The balog is officiated by two mediums, an elderly woman as the primary, and an elderly man as her assistant. No one is in full Ga'dang dress attire. The men are wearing daily G-strings or Western trousers; the women are wearing Western skirts and blouses, or traditional skirts with Western blouses. The boy is wearing short pants and a Western shirt, and the girl is wearing a Western dress.

Field notes, January 17, 1966, Cabanuangan

09:00   Just before the start of the ceremony, I notice that the old woman medium starts to gently strike an old Chinese porcelain bowl with a small stick. She chants as she strikes the bowl, as a way of getting the attention of the anitu so she can ask in a prayer that she be able to perform the balog properly so that the results will be positive. She asked that the boy and girl have a long and illness-free life. She is dressed in a traditional skirt and a Western-style blouse. On her head, she wears the *baginatnat*, a small headdress made from rattan.

10:30   The pig is tied by its feet to a bamboo pole and is being prepared to be killed. Since this is not a major ritual, the old woman does not pour water in the pig's ear to interpret its squeals and look for bad omens. If there was going to be a bad omen, she would have already seen it by now. Instead, a friend of the father inserts a long, thin knife in the jugular at the throat of the pig. The blood is allowed to flow into a metal pan. There is no real air of the "sacred" in this action. The mother of the boy and girl is pounding rice with some other women. Occasionally, the girl helps with the pounding. The father and the boy are standing and watching as the pig is killed.

Interpreting the sounds of a sacrificial pig, 1965.

11:00 Rice is cooking inside the house. Some men are preparing a hearth and fire where more rice will be cooked outside the house. There is also a fire for singeing the hair from the pig before it is scraped.

11:15 We are now going to the river with the carcass of the pig for butchering. I am with the father of the boy and girl, and four of his adult male friends. The pig is butchered by first removing the intestines and washing them, followed by removing the hips and shoulders, the head, and finally the ribs. The two mediums will each receive a shoulder or hip from the pig as payment for their services.

       After butchering, the father takes out two bottles of Black Hawk gin and squeezes bile from the pig's gallbladder into the bottles of gin. The mixture, said to prevent illness, is first offered to the anitu. "Share with the spirits and they will share with you." The lead butcher drinks some gin, followed by his assistant. The father then drinks the mixture. The rest of us then drink the mixture.

12:00 We have returned to the house where people have gathered to visit and eat and drink. Five large pots of rice are cooking outside of the house. The pork is being cut into smaller pieces and is being placed into pots for cooking. One pot is reserved for cooking the blood.

       The old woman medium appears to be supervising all the activities. The old man medium continues to chant.

12:45 For the past few minutes we have been visiting while eating small pieces of only slightly cooked pork. There is no order to who eats first. Most of us are milling about outside the house, including the two children for whom the balog is being held. The mother and father of the boy and girl, along with the two mediums, are inside the house. I notice that two men who live in Bananao are here for the ceremony, but they are not joining in the fun and are not eating or drinking. I am told that the son of the older man was recently murdered, so he and his friend are in mourning and are here to show respect for the father of the boy and the girl.

       Thus far, I have seen nothing, except for the few activities of the mediums, to suggest this event is anything more than a social event and an opportunity for the family to show they can afford the balog.

13:00 Four gong players have started playing. Often an older gong player will switch gongs with a younger player as if he is teaching the young man how to gong. There is some dancing by the men, including the gong players, but it is not done in earnest. It is more like a fun and practice session.

       The boy and girl who are being honored with the balog thus far have had no special activities. They do, however, appear to be walking around in a manner that suggests that they know the celebration is in their honor.

13:30 The old woman has started gently hitting her bowl again with the small bamboo and is praying. She is asking the anitu to guard over all that are present at the ceremony. A plate is placed before the old woman. Some beads belonging to the father and the mother of the boy and girl are placed on the plate. She prays again over the beads, again asking for good health for the children of the balog. Someone has killed a chicken and it is given to the old woman. The boy and girl move into the house and sit before the old woman. She takes some blood from the dead chicken and places a small amount on the forehead of the two children. She prays again. I am told that the children will be expected to dance for the crowd individually later this evening.

14:30   There are around 15 people here now, ready to eat and drink. We are all having a nice meal of rice and pork. The balog children have returned to playing with other children.

16:00   Everybody has been fed and had plenty to drink. It is time to rest before the social dance later this evening.

18:00   It's getting dark, and people are beginning to gather near the house of the balog. The gong players start to play their gongs. The pace is more rapid than other dances. The style tonight is mainly for individuals to dance, rather than groups of men or women. The gong players also dance and, once again, exchange gongs while playing. The dances are shorter than others I have seen . . . and more intense. Each dance lasts only about five minutes. The steps are quicker, the arms are more out-stretched, and the hands are always turned up.

19:00   The dance continues at the same rapid pace, with short stops between the dances. A few minutes ago, the two balog children stood in front of the house. The gong players gathered around them. Both children danced a short dance, and as the children danced, the gong players started to accelerate the beat of the gongs. They danced at the same time but danced as individuals. After about five minutes, the children returned to being children. Their parents watched with great pride and the crowd was highly appreciative of the children's dance, and of the food and the gin.

20:00   The event is about to end. The dancing has slowed, and people are beginning to go home. Others are chatting and drinking. It's time for me to rest.

Male mediums, especially at major ceremonies, such as an among or a key curing ceremony, performed specialized duties that complemented the activities of the female mediums. The men performed several duties, but their major activity was to chant what may be called the "Songs of the Mabayen." These songs, much more a chant than a song, were sung in slow, monotonous four-four time, with a singsong intonation by a mabayen during certain rituals. The only musical instrument accompanying the mabayen was a small drum made with the skin of a crocodile penis stretched across the opening of a short piece of bamboo. The mabayen thumped the small drum with his forefinger as he chanted. Occasionally, the mabayen would be assisted by a mukamong, and the chants were rendered in what the Ga'dang called the language of the anitu, an archaic form of Ga'dang not understood by most Ga'dang. In general, the chants relate mythical stories associated with important rituals, provide a rationale for the event, or dictate the ritual order of the event. These chants were sung from memory, and often they lasted for hours.

If the mabayen got tired, he would stop and rest. In the original study, the Ga'dang believed that certain rituals were incomplete without the songs of the mabayen.

The chants here were recorded in 1966. I could not find anyone during the restudy who could sing the chants. The older people had all heard the chants but could not identify anyone who could sing them. The chants were first translated from ritual Ga'dang into daily Ga'dang, and then into English. The translation is literal and unembellished. In a few cases, a ritual term could not be translated into daily Ga'dang even with the help of the mabayen and my Ga'dang helper. I believe we translated most of the lexemes correctly, but I may never know if we captured the intent and cultural significance of the chants. A short portion of a much longer chant follows. In this initial stanza of the chant, attention is directed to the importance of the number five and to chewing betel nut in rituals. The remaining stanzas, of which there are many, show how the seven anitu rituals previously discussed should be arranged and performed.

Respected mabayen, 1965.

kokanweno Alotu	The saying of Alotu
ma'lo masedan	I am possessed
lambutam i anak Awing	You might die my son
kokanweno Talangani	The saying of Talangani
i kanamak a Nanolay	I am like a relative of Nanolay
pagi sikwam Nanolay	You are not a relative of Nanolay
ginabat ti bilingan	Stand up Bilingan
dinomana gapatana	She took her basket
nesakama galab	Including the lid
netokina ki Alotu	She returned it to Alotu
bino'butna to'funa	He takes his betel nut bag
finisila balafiling	He holds the betel nut
sakama paratawetna	With the small knife
ne'almudna to apaanga	And other betel chewing things

nepalimanabsangat	Divided it into five pieces
nedijana makwolao	Included it with the betel leaf
sinarsikana aritangkang	Placing with the lime on the leaf
tufayang malabinggan	Small lime holder of bamboo tube
pitanda si'molan	First time putting the mixture in the mouth
pidwanda si'molan	Second time putting the mixture in the mouth
pi'wanda si'molan	Third time putting the mixture in the mouth
pipatanda si'molas	Fourth time putting the mixture in the mouth
balena pilimana	Finished at the fifth time
manganulang	Until
numatog bifida	Their lips become red
makanolan malaban	Spitting like a group
dinat ralura	Maya birds

Rituals: 2010–11

Although the Ga'dang of the restudy are Christian, subtle traditional Ga'dang beliefs persist such as believing that it is necessary to pay homage to a person's spouse, father, or mother on each anniversary of his or her death by placing some food and water on the grave. Mourning practices have been abandoned except that a person does not use a deceased close relative's name in a conversation, and mourning terms of respect are still used among older people.

There is one female medium living in Bananao. While she still maintains a small house with the unting hanging from the rafters, she no longer is involved in performing Ga'dang rituals. She says she is too old and very few people need her services today. When I asked her daughter why she never learned the way of the makamong, she said there was too much to learn, and it was too difficult. She said to me later, "There is no need now for a makamong."

There are no male mediums in Bananao.

Sickness and Health: 2010–11

Today, the closest part-time medical specialist to a makamong is the mafuyat. A mafuyat (often called a *hilot* by other Philippine groups) is a midwife who, in addition to her midwifery skills, practices a form of healing in which she places her hands and oil on the part of the patient's body that is "sick." As in the past, a person cannot say in Ga'dang, "I am sick." A person must specify the place of the "sickness," for example, "I am sick in the arm," "I am sick in the head," "I am sick with fever," and so forth. Once the area of the illness is identified by the mafuyat, she massages that part of the body. For her services, she receives a donation, the amount depending on the ability of the patient to pay.

The Ga'dang of the restudy have many of the same health issues their ancestors had: malaria, dengue fever, tuberculosis, glaucoma and cataract

A makamong with her grandchild, 1965 *(top)*.
The last makamong in Bananao with her daughter, 2010 *(bottom)*.

issues, diarrhea, stoke, influenza, pneumonia, and high fevers caused by unknown circumstances. Expressed linguistically, there is little difference between how the Ga'dang of the 1960s perceived illness from the Ga'dang of the present. Like so many aspects of change in the two studies, age is an important factor denoting general knowledge of illness, with those Ga'dang over the age of 40 better able to discuss health issues. When I asked younger Ga'dang about health issues, the general responses emphasized the importance of needing money in order to access the Philippine health system.

Different Ga'dang, depending on their education and travels, identify the causes of health problems in different ways. For most people, these health issues are attributed to the weather, dirty water, unclean food, or coming into contact with people who are ill. Often, illnesses are dismissed with the common Philippine concept of fatalism (Lieban 1966). Only people with some education associate germs with illness. Chronic conditions, such as malaria or acute febrile illness, may still be attributed to evil spirits, although instead of many spirits causing illness, the malevolent spirits now are limited to three or four. The most often discussed malevolent spirits today are aled, karangat, and bingil. A few Ga'dang still consider walking through the forest while tending to an uma cultivation plot to be a dangerous activity.

In 1965, I was sitting in a house with a group of Ga'dang when a man was suddenly stung by a scorpion. This man, usually very stoic, went into a panic. His behavior, especially his rolling on the floor and screaming, made me think he might die. I immediately rushed down the hill to the river and returned with a bowl of mud in which to pack his arm. Meanwhile, his wife called a medium/healer and she started to pray. She kept asking the anitu to stop the pain and for him not to die. After some discussion with the medium about whether a chicken should be sacrificed and what else to do, the mud I had placed on his arm was replaced with crushed freshwater shrimp. In about an hour his panic was gone, and except for his swollen arm, the event was over. His recovery was attributed to the prayers of the medium and the crushed shrimp.

If this man were stung by a scorpion today in Bayongyong, there would be no medium to call. Since there are no practicing mediums in Bananao now, spiritual healing has become an activity of the past. If the illness does not appear to be life threatening, often a person will go to the mafuyat, and she will administer her healing skills. She has some herbalist knowledge and has "hands-on" healing capabilities, but she does not perform any traditional rituals designed to heal. Sometimes, a Christian minister, or members of the ministry, will be asked to pray for a sick person, especially if the illness appears to be life threatening.

For the most part, when ill, a Ga'dang travels to the Poblacion to consult with a private physician (if he or she can afford one) or to see one of two physicians at the government hospital. (The poorer people of Bananao often do not receive medical attention due to the expense of traveling to the Poblacion and to the cost of medicine.) The hospital in the Poblacion has eight beds, a laboratory suitable only for limited blood and urine analysis, a small pharmacy, two physicians, and seven nurses/lab technicians. It has no X-ray machines. Occasionally a Ga'dang will travel to a large city in the Cagayan Valley to seek medical aid. The most important medical facility for the people of Bananao is the local government clinic.

The Bananao Clinic, a small cement block structure with three rooms, a cement floor and a galvanized roof, was established in 1993. It has no hospital beds except for one for prenatal examinations, and laboratory equipment is nonexistent. The clinic does not even have a simple blood-typing kit. The clinic is open five days a week and is staffed by one full-time registered nurse and one full-time registered and licensed midwife. There is also one volunteer midwife who works to gain experience in anticipation it will help her gain employment later. The nurse is an Ilocana and the two midwives are Ga'dang. All services are free to patients, but medicines must be purchased. If the needed medicines are unavailable in the clinic, a trip to either the Poblacion or the Cagayan Valley is necessary. The nurse cannot write prescriptions, but since most medicines (except those considered controlled substances) are sold across the counter in the Philippines, the nurse can make recommendations. A government physician is supposed to visit the Bananao Clinic once a month, but it is more likely the physician will visit once or twice a year.

The clinic is the government health services conduit to the local community. Consequently, the government often provides the clinic with flyers and posters detailing the preventative features of public health. For example, a large and prominent sign hangs in front of the clinic reminding all who pass by that malaria must be reported immediately to the local authorities. The sign, painted with bold lettering in Ilocano reads:

RAPID DIAGNOSTIC TEST OF MALARIA

1. Fever
2. Chills
3. Headache
4. Profuse Sweating

The clinic also has government-printed pamphlets on topics such as dengue fever, cleanliness, use of contraceptives, and bird flu that are passed out to patients.

Between 1 May 2010 and 31 May 2011, excluding inoculation visits for children, 441 people visited the Bananao Clinic. The average age was 22.6 years, with the youngest patient being two months old and the oldest patient being 70 years old. Only 11 percent of the visitors were males, while 89 percent of the visitors were females.

The 20 most common reasons given by patients for visiting the clinic and the nurse's recommendation during the restudy period are itemized below:

Most Common Reasons for Clinic Visits	Recommendation of the Nurse
Becoming pregnant too often	Use contraceptives
Sore eyes	Sunglasses, stay out of sun
General malaise	Check temperature and blood pressure
Dizziness	Check blood pressure
Headache	Check blood pressure and acetaminophen
Wound	Clean and bandage
Fever	Acetaminophen
Cough	Acetaminophen
Possible dengue fever	Refer to the Poblacion hospital
Infected wound	Clean, antibiotic ointment, and bandage
Infection from insect bites	Clean, antibiotic ointment, and bandage
Dog bite	Watch dog, clean, and wrap bite
General body pains	Check blood pressure, Vitamin C
Persistent runny nose	Vitamin C and acetaminophen
Diarrhea	Oral rehydration therapy
Anemia	Vitamins
Parasites	Education on cleanliness
Skin lesions	Topical antibiotic
Nervousness	Check blood pressure and vitamins

The government-recommended children's inoculations are BCG (tuberculosis), DPT 1, 2, 3 (diphtheria, tetanus and pertussis), polio 1, 2, 3, hepatitis B 1, 2, 3, and measles. On the third Wednesday of each month, the Bananao Clinic provides inoculations for children. This is a very busy day for the nurse and the midwives. Lines of women and children form as they wait for the nurse and midwife and their helpers to weigh infants, check for diseases, distribute government-provided medicines, and inoculate children. In addition to the medical services the clinic provides, clinic day is also a time where women gather from throughout the barangay to visit and catch up on the latest gossip.

Between May 2010 and May 2011, 47 live births were recorded for Barangay Bananao (27 males and 20 females). Of these 47 births, 12 (eight males and four females) were born to Ga'dang in Bayongyong. Eighty-three percent of these babies started the government-recommended series of inoculations, and after a year, 45 percent of them were still in the inoculation program. Clinic records suggest that 18 percent are no longer on an inoculation schedule. The others received some of the inoculations. While these figures for the Ga'dang compare favorably with the other ethnic groups in Bananao, there is a slight pattern suggesting that the farther away the mother is from the clinic, the greater the tendency to drop out of the inoculation program.

Inoculation day at the health clinic in Bananao, 2010.

Embracing Christianity: 1965–66 and 2010–11

Although the Ga'dang's rituals and view of the world were much the same in Pakak and Cabanuangan in the 1965–66 study, Christianity was beginning to penetrate the belief system of the Ga'dang living in Cabanuangan.

By 1965–66, some of the households in Cabanuangan had stopped putting unting in their houses. This allowed the members to disregard the taboo of eating corn and mudfish in the house. Corn was plentiful in the Cabanuangan area, and there were many mudfish in the nearby rice paddies. It is not that the Cabanuangan Ga'dang had been converted to Christianity—they had not—but some of their old beliefs were slowly being replaced by Christian ideas. For example, the creator deity of the Ga'dang, Nanolay, was becoming synonymous with the Spanish Dios—the Christian God. Later, with active proselytizing by Christian missionaries and Bible translators, the Ga'dang were told that Nanolay was Dios. It was a simple transition for the Ga'dang to make, so in time, Nanolay became Dios or God, and today, the term Nanolay is seldom heard, having been replaced by the term Dios It became convenient for the Christians to treat this difference in spiritual beings simply as a linguistic matter; doing so bypassed a fundamental Christian axiom, "Thou shall have no other gods before me" (Deuteronomy 5:7). Although equating Nanolay with God, especially in prayer, was a corruption of the Ga'dang tradition of addressing Nanolay—it was improper to say "I beg to Nanolay"—it fit the needs of missionaries and Bible translators. This subtle but fundamental erosion of Ga'dang culture may be illustrated with the following short prayer.

> *yo alakundakami ama a Jos si*
> *langit ta awan tacit ana awan matay.*
>
> Help us father God in heaven so there
> will be no sickness and no death.

Today, the term *Dios* (or *Jos* in the prayer) is used by the Ilocano to pray to the Christian God. *Langit* is the Ilocano term used to denote the Christian heaven. The idea of God as father (*ama a Jos*) would carry no meaning in traditional Ga'dang culture.

This move toward Christianity continued, and almost a half-century later the Ga'dang in Bananao are Christians, at least in some syncretistic form. There are five active Christian churches in Bananao: one Baptist, one Methodist, two Evangelical, and one Catholic. The least active church in Bananao is the Catholic Church. The Catholic priest visits only once or twice a month, sometimes less, and most of his parishioners are Ilocano. The most active ministries are the two evangelical churches. The Methodist and Baptist churches, while somewhat Pentecostal in orientation (the emphasis is on having a personal relationship with God through Baptism), are less so than the evangelical churches. Ga'dang attendance at church is sporadic. For example, one of the evangelical churches has a membership of 61. Yet, on any Sunday morning, there may be only 20 or 25 people at the service. The Wednesday night service may have as few as six to ten worshipers. The minister's formal relationship with a national church organization will condition whether he receives compensation for his ministry. All of the ministers in Bananao have some farming responsibilities.

Importantly, most of the Ga'dang want all to know that they are Christian. In fact, there is a tendency on the part of most Ga'dang to equate "non-Christian" with "uncivilized," and nobody wants to be known as "uncivilized." One middle-aged woman who had worked as a domestic in Hong Kong and was defensive about some of my questions about Christianity in Bananao said to me in forceful English, "I'm a civilized woman. . . . I'm a liberated woman! I'm a Christian."

Protestantism, especially as practiced in churches that are Pentecostal in belief and charismatic in practice (speaking in tongues, receiving gifts from God, and being possessed by the Holy Spirit), have a long, complicated, and controversial history in the Philippines (Anderson and Tang 2005; Lumahan 2005). The arrival of Protestantism coincides with possession of the Philippines by the United States in 1898. The Baptists, Presbyterians, and Methodists were the first Protestants to meet and sign a comity agreement in which they agreed on how to divide the Philippines into different mission territories in 1898. During the following ten years, a few more mission denominations joined this coalition, but after a Filipino broke with the Methodist Church in 1909 and founded an indigenous Christian Church, the comity agreement fell into disuse. Soon, the country was hosting hundreds of Protestant missionaries, and indigenous Christian Churches were established in many sections of the country. More than 100 Pentecostal charismatic groups, ministries, or churches were formed in the Philippines after 1960 (Lumahan 2005:339).

While there were Christian missionaries along the Cordillera Central in earlier years, the push to convert the minorities of the area to Protestantism began soon after World War II and reached its most active point during the late 1960s and early 1970s. By this time in the Paracelis area, especially near the Poblacion, locally trained Filipino evangelical missionaries had set up operations. In addition, representatives of SIL International (a Christian-language research organization) and its sister group Wycliffe International (a Bible translating organization) were established in Paracelis. According to informants in Bayongyong, it was during this period that the Ga'dang started to convert to Christianity, even though technically the Bible translators were not missionaries.

The Evangelical Church in Bayongyong, 2010.

The acceptance of Jesus Christ followed by baptism in the river became the norm for the Ga'dang, especially in the 1970s. Even some of the oldest Ga'dang were baptized during the late 1970s. Sometimes they converted because their children who had converted asked them to "join the church." One elderly Ga'dang man replied to my question on why he became a Christian with, "I changed when I learned that the Ga'dang way is the Devil's way." A few Ga'dang report that a small number of evangelistic ministers became so animated in the frenzy of converting the Ga'dang to Christianity they insisted the converts burn their traditional clothing. One minister tried to get some of his Ga'dang converts to throw away their beads because they were a symbol of their "pagan ways." This was too great an economic sacrifice for the converts. Numerous Ga'dang with whom I discussed the Christianizing activities of the 1970s told me that it was the Filipino Pentecostal missionaries who were the more active and aggressive of the missionaries.

While the Spanish used the sword to convert the indigenous people of the Philippines to Christianity, the evangelical Protestants took a more psychological approach—mainly they made promises of rewards and punishments—stimulating the Ga'dang to convert to Christianity. As rewards they gave away medicines, used clothing, food, and in a few cases, money and land, and they promised each household a Christian Bible and a rich and better life in heaven. All the Ga'dang had to do was accept Dios as their Savior and to be baptized. And, of course, if the Ga'dang did not accept Christianity, they would be damned to a place called "hell," a place the Ga'dang had never heard of prior to the arrival of the Christians.

The Ga'dang received a printed Christian Bible in 2000 entitled *Ino Sapiti Dios* (Bible League 2000). This may be translated into English as "The Word of God." A survey of Christian Bibles on the Internet or at the university library shows that most Christian Bible translations have the word "Bible," "Holy Bible," or some literal translation of "Bible" imprinted on the front and spine of the printed book. This is not the case with the Ga'dang Bible; imprinted on the cover is "The Word of God" in Ga'dang. The commitment of the Bible translators to converting "pagans" to Christians seems clear in this title.

With the establishment of Christianity in the Paracelis area, Ga'dang ritual and spiritual life began to change. It has changed so much over the past 45 years that it is hardly recognizable today as Ga'dang.

In Bananao, I could find only two houses in which the house *unting* hang, one of which is no longer used, but stands as a testament to the Ga'dang belief system of the past. Compared to the 1965–66 study, a house in which a Ga'dang family lives today is no longer a Ga'dang home. The house-building ritual is not performed, young people do not know what the house *unting* are, and the taboos formerly associated with the Ga'dang house have disappeared. One of the Ga'dang "homes" in Bananao belongs to a woman probably around 90 years of age, and who was once a very active medium. She no longer practices her craft. The other Ga'dang "home" belongs to an elderly couple who are probably in their 80s. When I asked informants about the unting, if they recognize the term, most looked at me and said, "It is an old superstition."

The seven anitu rites of the Ga'dang that were so important in the past are no longer practiced. In fact, informants do not remember with any clarity when the last anitu was held.

As noted, by 1966, especially in Cabanuangan, the Ga'dang mythological creator Nanolay was becoming synonymous with the Spanish Dios for some Ga'dang, and as noted, today, Nanolay is considered God. Very few Ga'dang are aware that Nanolay (except as God rather than as Nanolay) was the creator of the world. Except for a very few elderly Ga'dang, the idea that the world was created by a rat is laughable. The concept of anitu for all practical purposes is lost to the Ga'dang. Even when aware that a certain myth exists, like so many other traditional beliefs, people dismiss it as superstition.

As noted, an important Ga'dang concept of the past was kalekay, which was one-half of the total world of ilosa, with the other half being the dufafa. Traditionally the Ga'dang had no concept of heaven and hell—there was kalekay (the up-after world) and dufafa (the earth world). Both worlds were very similar. In the restudy, both heaven and hell figure prominently in the worldview of the Ga'dang. A person is rewarded with heaven for living a good life, accepting Jesus Christ as Savior, and being baptized by immersion. Anything less and the person will burn in hell for eternity.

Except for the Christian theological beliefs associated with death and afterlife, Ga'dang funerals as performed today are similar to those of the past. When a person dies, neighbors come to the aid of the spouse. Sometimes a small hut is constructed for the body, but more often, the body remains in the house and is placed on a bench for viewing by friends and relatives. As in the past, the casket is made from bamboo or wood by neighbors, and the grave is dug. Today, unlike in the past, a local part-time embalmer is called to inject the body. The deceased is dressed in her or his best clothes. If the family can afford it, food is prepared for the guests, and a Christian minister is paid to pray and oversee the funeral. Many families, however, cannot afford the costs of a funeral. Just before the casket is closed and lowered with rope into a six-foot-deep grave and the grave is covered, a change of clothes and food are placed in the casket. If the family can afford it, the casket may be placed into a cement tomb. Occasionally, a personal item such as a walking stick or a betel nut bag is placed on the grave and retrieved by a family member later.

Except that membership is larger in one of the two nondenominational churches in Bayongyong and that church building is larger and made from cement blocks, overall, the rituals and organization of the two churches are the same. There is a church service on Sunday mornings and a prayer meeting on Wednesday evenings. For purposes of illustrating contemporary Ga'dang spiritual rituals in Bayongyong, a Sunday morning service is presented, as follows:

The ritual is held in a cement-block building approximately ten meters wide and 20 meters long, with a galvanized roof, and a cement floor. There is a locally made pulpit at the head of the room, and a wooden cross hangs on the wall behind the pulpit. The seating area for the congregation consists of plastic chairs. The building has four glassless windows, two on each side of the building.

In this service, the room is crowded, with 19 adult participants (not including nine toddlers). All the adults are women except for six men, and of these six, one is the pastor, one is the assistant pastor, three are church elders, and I am one. The service is held mainly in Ilocano, with some Ga'dang and an occasional English phrase or two. Music is provided by one of the church elders who plays an electric guitar. Everyone is dressed in nonwork clothes as best he or she can afford. The demeanor of the participants is casual, and the toddlers are allowed to wander and play, as they want. Three dogs repeatedly enter and leave the room. A couple of young women are breast-feeding.

The service started around 8:30 AM and ended around noon.

The Christian Bible used in the service was written in Ilocano. I asked the pastor why they used an Ilocano Bible in a Ga'dang service, and he replied, "We all speak Ilocano here and we prefer the Ilocano Bible. Besides, we think the Ilocano Bible is a much better translation than the Ga'dang Bible."

The service is divided into two parts, and is similar to an American Christian church service consisting of a Sunday school portion followed by an address by the pastor, except in this church both activities take place in a single room. In addition to the dichotomy between the first and second parts of the ritual, with the assistant pastor leading the first part and the pastor leading the second part, the service may be further segregated into six sections: (1) welcome address, (2) testimonies to God, (3) singing performance, (4) church offering, (5) the sermon, and (6) public announcements.

The service commences with an opening welcome by the assistant pastor and a prayer, followed by him bringing to the attention of the congregation the lesson for the week. The lesson for the week is "Be ready for God's Coming." To convey the lesson of the week, the assistant pastor reads a passage from Thessalonians 4–5, followed by the next verse being read aloud by a woman from the congregation. This is repeated several times. The opening welcome is followed by the congregation singing several songs, the most notable to a Western ear, "What a Friend We Have in Jesus," is sung in Ilocano.

The congregational singing is followed by a performance by the youth choir, consisting of four teenage girls and one boy (who do not stay for the remainder of the service). They sing four songs in Ilocano and English, the most rousing of which is "Jesus Set Me Free."

The next part of the ceremony is a series of spontaneous testimonials by the participants recounting God's blessings on them for the week. One woman is thankful for a safe trip to Bontoc to visit relatives. One man is thankful that God has blessed him with a new grandchild during the week. Many people offer thanks to God, most having to do with health, crops, and safety. The testimonials are reminiscent of the rather lengthy oratory challenges (lacking boasting) that characterized some Ga'dang rituals of the 1965–66 study.

The testimonials are followed by a basket being passed from person to person as the assistant pastor offers a prayer of thanks for what the church is about to receive. People are very careful to hold their contribution in such as way that others cannot see the amount placed in the basket.

The pastor welcomes the congregation, offers a prayer, and proceeds with his sermon. Following up on the lesson for the day, the sermon is based on the first letter of Paul to the Thessalonians in which he informs his followers that only people who have given themselves to God will be accepted into Heaven when the world comes to an end. The sermon is well organized and focuses on two themes: "The Lord Is Coming" and "Be Ready for the Lord's Coming." The pastor describes the reasons for the letters of Paul to the Thessalonians and focuses on how to be a good Christian. Perhaps it is the pastor's style, but there is a minimum of fundamentalist rhetoric associated with the sermon. Throughout the hour sermon, I hear no more than five "amens" spontaneously shouted from the congregation. I think the Ga'dang man sitting behind me senses I am having difficulty following the sermon, so he offers me a Bible with Ilocano printed in one column, paired with English in a parallel column.

The pastor ends his sermon with a prayer related to the Lord teaching his followers how to be good Christians and with a prayer related to the lesson of the day and his sermon of the day. The final activity of the service is theologically anticlimactic: there are public announcements by the assistant pastor related to future community activities.

Chapter 7

What's in a Word?

Measuring Culture Change

ℱew writers have more cogently presented the case for culture as patterned behavior than A. L. Kroeber (1948:311–343) in his classic textbook entitled *Anthropology,* much of which is as relevant today as it was over 60 years ago (see Chick 2000). Kroeber's discussion of what he called "systemic culture patterns" is especially germane here because as he noted, "It is already clear that understanding of culture as something more than an endless series of haphazard items is going to be achieved largely through recognition of patterns and our ability to analyze them" (1948:336). As further noted by Kroeber, "What distinguishes these systemic patterns of culture—or well patterned systems, as they might also be called—is a specific interrelation of their component parts, a nexus that holds them together strongly, and tends to preserve their basic plan" (1948:312–313).

As shown in earlier chapters, measuring the changes in Ga'dang culture since 1965–66 by noting the presence or absence of a cultural attribute or concept, whether dramatic or subtle, is a relatively uncomplicated measurement of change. For example, in the realm of patterns found in material culture, the fact that Ga'dang men no longer wear a G-string, except maybe at an occasional municipal fiesta, is easily observable and measurable. In matters of social behavior, the absence of the practice of spouse exchange reflects much broader systemic changes in social patterns associated with the diminished need for the expansion of a person's circle of kin. In culture domains associated with religious or spiritual behavior, measuring change becomes more complicated. For example, the conceptual change associated with the behavioral change of never praying to Nanolay and then to the metamorphic conversion of Nanolay into the Christian God is more subtle but is, nonetheless, measurable.

117

In this chapter, I go beyond the measurement of the presence or absence of cultural behaviors, items, or events. My concern is the measurement of cultural concepts and patterns that are far more subtle than whether or not the cultural trait or event is present or absent.

Methods

In developing a method for measuring culture change, I have drawn theoretical concepts from the fields of comparative linguistics, ethnoscience, and the study of systemic culture patterns. This is done in an attempt to determine more clearly the extent to which Ga'dang culture has changed since 1965–66.

In the comparative linguistic discipline of lexicostatistics, a "culture free" or "universally used" core set of terms such as "head," "foot," "sky," "many," "louse," "fire," "one," and "animal" are compared to determine lexical cognates (cf. Dyen 1975; Hymes 1960; Swadesh 1950, 1955, 1971) for purposes of measuring the relationships between languages in the present or through time. Obviously since language is a human activity, there are no "culture-free" words, but there are words in most languages that represent a universality of things and activities that reflect humans and human environments. Rather than measuring the percentage of cognates between two languages to determine linguistic divergence, here I use concepts as expressed in language use to determine the extent to which the Ga'dang perceived cultural concepts in 1965–66 differently than they did in 2010–11.

In the language-based cultural concepts measurement approach here, instead of using culture-universal terms—such as hand, foot, dog, egg, sleep, die, fire, water, and other universal concepts expressed in all cultures—I use what may be called "culture-constrained" or "culture-biased" or even "culturally-loaded" terms to measure culture change, at least culture change as expressed in language use. No attempt is made here to assign a rate of change to the results. Moreover, the words are the opposite of culture-universal terms and are dependent on culture for definition and understanding. For example, in English, the term "jitterbug" is a culturally constrained term, and although there may be some individual interpretation of "jitterbug" for English speakers, it probably holds a similar meaning for English speakers living in the 1940s and for those living in the present. It is possible to compare one person's meaning of jitterbug with the way another person might use the same term. In Ga'dang, the term *"abafini"* ("the rice growing season") might be interpreted differently by some Ga'dang speakers because it is inclusive of a range of planting behaviors. Importantly, however, all adult Ga'dang speakers in my 1965–66 study would have recognized the broad ramifications of the term.

The terms used here were present in spoken Ga'dang in 1965–66 and are taken directly from my field notes. I am comparing the Ga'dang's understanding of a concept in 1965–66 with their understanding of the same concept in the present. I compare "knowledge of" rather than the actual term or concept. I measure the way individuals understand the term in 2010 as compared to their understanding of the term in 1965. It is the patterns of change as expressed in the way the Ga'dang of today perceive their cultural world as compared to the way the Ga'dang of 1965–66 viewed their cultural world that is the focus of my concern. My aim is to measure the extent to which the Ga'dang have lost traditional cultural knowledge as expressed in the use of their language over the past 45 years.

From the field of ethnoscience, even with consideration for the criticisms leveled at the method (cf. Berreman 1966; Burling 1964; Frake 1964b; Goodenough 1956; Harris 1979; Sanga and Ortalli 2004; Spradley 1972, 1979; Tyler 1969; Wallace 1983), the approach followed here adheres to the theory that people perceive their world through the cognitive categories of the language they speak. This approach helps to bring order to my analysis of changes in Ga'dang culture. In particular, the concept of culture domain—a cognitive category that includes other categories—is utilized to classify behavior. To reduce the use of non-English terms, and for purposes of clarification and presentation, I include some Ga'dang lexemes under English domains.

From the study of systemic culture patterns and reliability testing in the social sciences, I utilize the concept of "high-concordance codes" (Chick 2000) to improve the reliability of ethnographic analysis. But, instead of measuring intracultural sharing (Romney and Moore 1998), I measure cultural sharing in the same culture at two different points in time. As used here, high-concordance codes are patterned nomenclatures or sets of terms—single terms or phrases that denote particular concepts (Roberts et al. 1971:244–245).

Measuring Change

Twenty-five culture-based concepts, some of which are culture domains and some of which are categories of a domain, were selected from my 1965–66 Ga'dang field notes for the interview schedule. All adult Ga'dang in Pakak and Cabanuangan in 1965–66 would have had knowledge of these concepts—the concepts were commonly used in 1965–66. This is not to deny that even in smaller and more isolated communities some individuals have a larger specialized vocabulary than other individuals. For example, a senior Ga'dang male might possess a more detailed vocabulary associated with hunting than a novice hunter. Some societies, of course, are known to possess an extraordinary vocabulary associated with certain aspects of life. For example, Robert Fox (1953) demonstrates how the Pinatubo Aeta of the Philippines possessed a phenomenal knowledge of the relationships between their plant and animal worlds. Even Pinatubo Aeta children used a plant/animal taxonomic vocabulary much more extensively than their neighboring ethnic groups.

There are numerous Ga'dang concepts from my 1965–66 study that I could have chosen to design the measuring instrument, but in order to keep the interview schedule manageable, twenty-five lexemes or words were selected for analysis. All 25 of the lexemes were known and were used often by the adult Ga'dang in the 1965–66 study. These words were not specialized or exotic and were used with the same basic meaning by all adult Ga'dang in the 1965–66 study. The 25 Ga'dang terms are organized into the broadly based anthropological categories representing (1) Spiritual Concepts, (2) Social Concepts, (3) Environmental Concepts, and (4) Other Concepts. Forty percent of the terms represent concepts depicting spiritual behavior, 32 percent represent aspects of social behavior, 12 percent pertain to environmental categories, and 16 percent are lexemes that do not fall into any of these categories.

Spiritual Concepts include behavior based on Ga'dang worldview and on ritual practices associated with the afterworld, spirits, souls, and magic. Social Concepts reflect behavior associated with marriage, kinship, and rites of passage. Environmental Concepts are associated with the reality of the environment where the Ga'dang lived in 1965–66. While some of the lexemes are conceptual categories in Ga'dang, they are less so in English. For example, the term *"talun"* in Ga'dang is a domain made up of several different types of forest. Other Concepts are lexemes that are significant to the Ga'dang but do not fit into a particular category unless a full culture-domains analysis is undertaken. The twenty-five lexemes, based on descriptions provided by Ga'dang during the 1965–66 study, are described briefly below.

- **Spiritual Concepts.** *Nanolay,* the creator of the world who figures prominently in Ga'dang mythology; *anitu,* an indefinable spirit that served as a go-between for humanity and Nanolay and the up-after world, and certain rituals promoted by Nanolay; *kararawa,* the soul of a man, a woman, or animals such as pigs, deer, or birds; *kalekay,* the up-after world where all creatures go after death; *unting,* a set of inter-related concepts endowing extraordinary power to objects; *incanto,* malevolent magic; *aran,* a malevolent spirit that appeared in the forest in the form of a mist; *bingil,* distorted human-like ghouls, often having only one eye; *karangat,* a malevolent spirit that could transform itself into almost any form, and was responsible for making people insane; *aled,* the lost soul of an ancestor.

- **Social Concepts.** *inafafu,* distant ancestors representing a bilateral kin group; *pangit,* a kinship term of address or reference for widower; *among,* a set of social rites of passage promoting good health and social status; *waiyi,* general kin terms for relatives; *panganakan,* kinship term of reference for nephew or niece; *balog,* the first of the among, held when the person is a small child; *tolay,* a general term meaning man or woman or "the people"; *solyad,* the practice of spouse exchange.

- **Environmental Concepts.** *alifambang,* a general term for any type of butterfly; *lamag,* a crocodile; *talun,* a particular type of forest.

- **Other Concepts.** *gured,* scabies, but occasionally applied to any type of skin disease; *galating,* a musical instrument made from bamboo and played often during social dances; *sillay,* a general gloss for beads, both ordinary and special beads; *lufay,* a culturally prescribed type of earring used in numerous rituals and economic transactions.

In establishing the categories, my assumption was that the closer the concept was to being a culture universal, the less likely the speakers of the language would lose or modify the meaning of the term in a period of time of only 45–50 years. While estimates for the rate of language change vary greatly—for example, 4–14 percent per millennium for Icelandic and Norwegian (Chapman 1962)—language usage does reflect culture change. Therefore, I expected that a term like alifambang (butterfly) would be more likely to persist in the vocabulary unmodified than a clearly culturally based concept such as solyad or karangat. The core of the interview schedule is the Spiritual Concepts and the Social Concepts. The Environmental Concepts and the Other Concepts are included in the interview schedule mainly as a check and balance of the obvious. This is why 72 percent of the lexemes in the interview schedule are from the spiritual and social domains of Ga'dang culture, while only 28 percent of the lexemes are from the less culturally based aspects of Ga'dang culture.

The interview schedule was conducted in spoken Ga'dang and consisted of asking the respondent a simple and straightforward question: *"On Taranu* _____?" In English, this question translates as "What does _____ mean to you?" Occasionally, with a younger respondent, it was necessary to ask the same question in Ilocano, which is *"Ipalawag* _____?" or *"Ilawlawag* _____?" In some cases, the respondent would answer the question in Ga'dang, sometimes in English or Ilocano, and occasionally in a combination of Ga'dang, Ilocano, and English.

The interview schedule was administered to 50 adults representing 50 different households, all Ga'dang, and all living in the barangay of Bananao. This is a 27 percent sample of the Ga'dang households in Bananao. The sample was further divided into males and females, and into the age grades of 20–29, 30–39, 40–49, 50–59, and over 60 years of age. Five men and five women were interviewed from each age group.

The response to each concept was weighted with a numerical score. The scoring system, which was measured against the common way the terms were used and understood by the Ga'dang in the 1965–66 study, follows. One important Ga'dang concept—Nanolay—will serve as an example of how I scored the answers to my questions:

- *Five points:* The respondent has a full understanding of the concept as articulated during the 1965–66 study; e.g., the respondent understands and articulates that Nanolay is a deity and the creator of the world.

- *Four points:* The respondent understands the concept, but with sufficient conceptual variation to indicate some loss or change of knowledge or understanding; e.g., the respondent can identify Nanolay as a deity, but does not recognize that Nanolay is a mythical character, who among other things, created the world.

- *Three points:* The respondent recognizes the concept, but is unable to articulate its significance within the culture; e.g., the respondent can identify Nanolay as a creature of the spirit world, but is unable to elaborate further.
- *Two points:* The respondent has heard of Nanolay, but is unable to discuss the concept except in vague spirit world terms.
- *One point:* The respondent has heard of Nanolay but lacks an understanding of its significance; e.g., the respondent recognizes the term Nanolay, but places it in an incorrect domain.
- *Zero points:* The respondent has a total misunderstanding of the concept as used in 1965; e.g., the respondent does not recognize Nanolay or the respondent answers the question with "I do not know," e.g., the respondent states that he or she does not know the term Nanolay.

This is not a perfect scoring system and is interpretive on my part. There probably would be some variation in scoring if two researchers with dissimilar backgrounds were to undertake the scoring task. Conversely, if two researchers with similar backgrounds did the scoring, the variation would be diminished. In the situation here, the conceptual language data were collected by me in 1965–66, and the interview schedule was designed, administered, and scored by me in 2010–11. Given the passage of almost 50 years and the work being done in the field setting, the reliability control seems reasonable.

Following this scoring system, the highest score a respondent can receive is 5 times 25 or 125 points. The lowest score a respondent can receive is 0 times 25 or 0 points. If a respondent, for example, receives a score of 76 (60.8 percent), he or she will have received a culture knowledge score, as expressed in language use, assuming a perfect score in 1965–66 was 100 percent. This score also could be considered a 39 percent loss of cultural knowledge as expressed through language use since the 1965–66 study. It should be emphasized that unless the respondent is over 45 years of age, he or she was not born at the time of the 1965–66 study. Or, if the respondent was 15 years old—roughly the onset of Ga'dang adulthood—at the time of the 1965–66 study, he or she would now be 60 years old. This is important because, as already noted, the 1960s and 1970s were a time of rapid environmental, social, and cultural change along the Cordillera Central.

Patterns of Culture Change

In the analysis that follows, it should be noted that the differences between 1965–66 and the present reflect changes in Ga'dang perception as expressed in language use. Without assessing the complexity of the principle of linguistic relativity (Kay and Kempton 1984; Lucy 1997), it is assumed here that language, language use, and language retention influences behavior and reflects cultural knowledge. Therefore, the following analysis is a reasonable indicator of changes in cultural patterns among the Ga'dang between the years 1965 and 2011.

The general results from the interview schedule show that over the past 45 years, the Ga'dang, at least those living in the Bananao area, have retained a 77 percent understanding of all the cultural concepts contained in the interview schedule. This general figure, however, requires further analysis. If the understanding and retention of a cultural concept is calculated based on categories of concepts, a different and more informative pattern emerges. From the total sample, regardless of age or sex, the Ga'dang have retained an understanding of 50 percent of their Spiritual Concepts. They have retained a 65 percent understanding of their Social Concepts. Since these categories are more abstract and intangible, and require a fuller understanding of Ga'dang culture than more culture-universal terms, the conceptual scores are relatively low. In the categories of Environmental and Other Concepts, the Ga'dang have retained a 97 percent and a 96 percent understanding (see figure 5).

Considering that the Environmental and Other categories are comprised of words that reflect the immediate surrounding (e.g., butterfly, forest, scabies, and beads, etc.), the high retention rate is expected. Except for the symbolism associated with Ga'dang beads, the other terms in these categories may reflect little more than the Ga'dang still speak Ga'dang. For example, all respondents were able to identify "butterfly," and "crocodile," even though there are no longer any crocodiles in the Ga'dang area. All respondents but one were able to identify "*galating*" (musical instrument made from bamboo), even though galating are seldom used today.

The differences in the degree of change and the understanding and retention of all the concepts in the interview schedule become more significant when the calculations are based on age. As noted, any respondent over the age of 60 was a least 15 years of age at the time of the 1965–66 study. They had already matured into young men and women and were well into the enculturation process of being a Ga'dang. If the scores associated with Environmental and Others Concepts are factored out of the tabulations, the changes are even more dramatic (see figures 6 and 7).

Two women, one 88 years old and the other 72 years old, each received a score of 84 percent for all categories in the interview schedule, the highest of all scores. The 72-year-old woman grew up in the Paracelis area. The 88-year-old woman moved to Bayongyong in the late 1960s from Pakak. I had known her when she was in her early 40s. A 25-year-old male scored 49 percent, the lowest of all scores. If his scores pertaining to the environment and other concepts were eliminated, his score would have been much lower. Two noteworthy inconsistencies merit further discussion. Despite that fact that spouse exchange (solyad) is no longer practiced by the Ga'dang, 100 percent of the respondents were able to articulate the concept, a culturally based practice with numerous social ramifications. The responses varied—some said that it was adultery, some said it was an old Ga'dang custom, and others fully understood the concept—but it was clear that all respondents knew of the

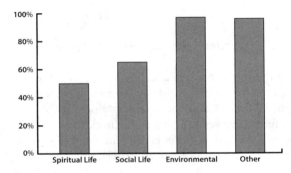

Figure 5   Retention of Cultural Concepts, 1965–2011

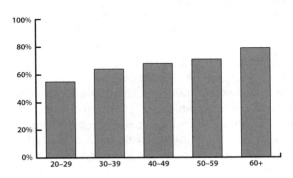

Figure 6   Retention of Cultural Concepts by Age, 1965–2011

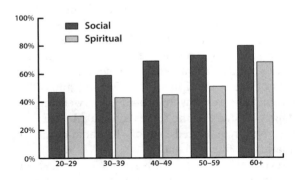

Figure 7   Retention of Social and Spiritual Concepts by Age, 1965–2011

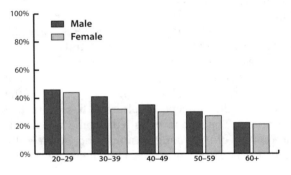

Figure 8   General Loss of Cultural Concepts by Age and Gender, 1965–2011

concept. A possible interpretation of this contradiction rests in the fact that occasionally a piously Christian Ga'dang will hold up the practice of spouse exchange as how not to act, or point out that spouse exchange is, as one man said, "uncivilized" behavior. Similarly, although most Ga'dang women no longer own or wear the traditional necklaces of beads, all respondents were able to identify *sillay* as Ga'dang strings of beads. This is less a contradiction, however, than it might appear because most Ga'dang still consider beads as a cultural marker identifying a person as Ga'dang.

It is clear that language changes through time, but the critical issue is how does language change reflect cultural behavior? In the case of the Ga'dang, the changes in cultural knowledge as expressed through language are reasonably clear. In Bananao, for example, people over 50 years of age grew up in a culturally homogeneous Ga'dang community (with some general cultural variation based on age, sex, and interests) and the primary language spoken was Ga'dang, except when men were away trading in the lowlands. Very few Ga'dang in Bananao over the age of 50 have as much as an elementary education.

People in the restudy under 30 years of age grew up in culturally heterogeneous villages; they grew up speaking Ga'dang, Ilocano, and some English; and most of them attended at least some high school. Consequently, in cultural concepts associated with social and spiritual behavior, although Ga'dang over 50 years of age scored significantly higher than Ga'dang of age 30 or less, neither age group approach having the knowledge that was commonly held by adults in 1965. If the cultural concepts—expressed in language use—are absent or limited, the behavior will be absent or limited. It is clear that the loss of cultural concepts, along with numerous environmental, economic, and political factors, have served to erode traditional Ga'dang culture and behavior and stimulate new or modified expressions of Ga'dang culture and behavior (see figure 8).

Although some important cultural concepts have been modified, discarded, or lost to the younger Ga'dang, and Ilocano and other languages are spoken in the area, Ga'dang is still the language of the Ga'dang. As a way of testing for the basic retention of spoken Ga'dang, I asked Ga'dang of different age groups for the descriptive terminology associated with the human body. I chose this terminological system because it represents culturally universal categories (body parts), but it is not totally culture-free. Unlike in the study of cultural concepts, I am more concerned with if people recognize the words rather than if they possess cultural knowledge associated with the term. While not all Ga'dang had command of the complete set of body terms, in general, people over 40 had greater familiarity with the body parts than people under 30. If the same body parts questions were asked in English from a high school graduate in the United States, the range of variation in recognition probably would not differ significantly.

In addition to the changes expressed through the presence and absence of Ga'dang cultural patterns associated with the environment, economy, social and spiritual life, changes may also been expressed through changes in perceptions as expressed through language use. Clearly, Ga'dang over the age of 50 perceive the world differently from Ga'dang age 50 and under. As expressed in the retention of the knowledge of Ga'dang culture, this is especially note-worthy in the cultural areas of social life and spiritual life (see figure 7).

In conjunction with the drawings of a domestic pig, I asked the question, phrased in Ga'dang, of "What are the 'necessary' parts of the body?" The responses were *ule* (complete head), *ta'gang* (chest area), *bu'lao* (complete neck area), *langalay* (complete arm), *daruru* (back area), *patung* (hip area),

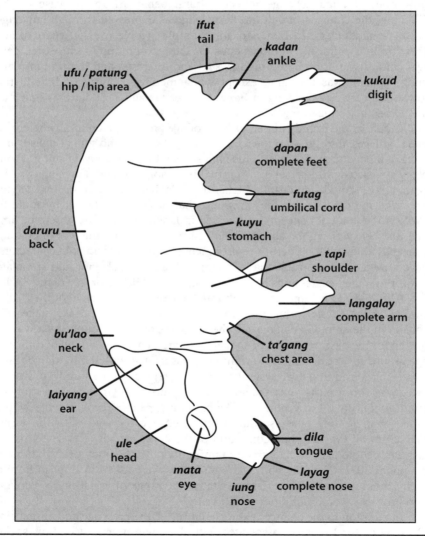

Figure 9 Pig Drawing Showing Body-Part Terminology

dapan (complete foot), and *kamat* (complete hand). Assuming the body parts exist, this terminology can apply to animals, such as a pig or water buffalo, or to a human, but, for example, not to a fish or a turtle. If there is a right and a left to the body part, this must be expressed with a right or left designation.

After obtaining the basic parts of the body, the follow-up question was, "What are the 'necessary' parts of the head?" The answer was *abok* (hair on top of head), *kiri* (forehead), *kimat* (eye brows and/or eye lashes), *mata* (complete eye), *layag* (complete nose), *abut na iyung* (hole in the nose), *paringel* (upper and lower lips), *iming* (chin or cheek hair), *dila* (tongue), *damuan* (front teeth), *bangid* (canine teeth), *atong* (jaw teeth), *wangit* (complete mouth), *utak* (brain), *tantel* (back of head), *biki* (complete skull or any of the larger skull bones), and *dalamit* (temple area of the skull).

This approach, designed to elicit Ga'dang body terminology, was then extended to include more detailed body parts, including internal organs. All adult Ga'dang, both younger and older, were able to answer my questions, with few difficulties, when presented in this orderly manner. In daily spoken Ga'dang, there appears to be little loss of language, at least in areas needed for daily interaction. As noted, the culture loss is most dramatic in culturally based concepts related to gods, spirits, and some social institutions. Ga'dang culture may be rapidly eroding, but spoken Ga'dang remains relatively intact, at least in the less conceptual and less abstract domains of culture.

Chapter 8

The Inevitability of Change

Summary and Conclusions

*T*here is a term in Ga'dang—*napayot*—that may be translated as "to become like," "to change into," or "become the other." In spoken Ga'dang, napayot represents what may be identified for purposes here as the principle of the inevitability and acceptance of change. Since my original study in 1965, the Ga'dang seldom have resisted change. In a few cases, some Ga'dang have embraced change, others acknowledge the inevitability of change, and most Ga'dang have accepted change as an adaptive strategy for living in a modern world. For the Ga'dang, change is inevitable. The Ga'dang view of change may be summarized in the following statements from three different Ga'dang, two men and a woman, living in Bayongyong.

> "We Ga'dang have stopped living our way of life and language, and have accepted the ways of another tribe."

> "We have left our olden ways of living."

> "The Ilocano are the most successful here so we want to do what they do."

The statements by these three elderly persons should not be interpreted to mean that the Ga'dang are a "defeated" ethnic group or are a "sad story," as illustrated by the Batak, traditionally a tropical forest foraging (and sometimes kaingin cultivating) people living on the Philippine island of Palawan, eloquently discussed by James Eder in his *On The Road to Tribal Extinction* (1987). For the Batak and some other tribal groups in the Philippines and Southeast Asia, the erosion of language and culture, changes in the environment, and the penetration of outsiders into the community greatly affected the well-being of the people and their ability to cope with the stress these factors created. In Eder's words, "I believe a direct, causal relationship exists between the ero-

129

sion of Batak ethnic identity (and the sense of coherence it provided in their lives) and the desultory nature of Batak material life" (1987:241).

It would appear that the Batak, to use a popular anthropological phrase, have been "victims of progress," although as Eder demonstrates, this is a great oversimplification of the processes of change. Conversely, the Ga'dang reacted differently than the Batak to similar changes. If the loss of language and culture is the measuring instrument determining the extent to which a group is a victim of progress, then the Ga'dang have been victims of progress. The Ga'dang, however, do not perceive themselves as victims of progress. Instead, they perceive themselves as a people who accept, sometimes reluctantly, the inevitability of change. Although certainly not all Ga'dang welcome such changes, they work to insure as smooth a transition through change as possible. Utilizing their limited resources, they have worked to integrate themselves into the political economy of Northern Luzon (cf. Fox et al 2009; Edelman and Haugerud 2005; Popkin 1979).

It is clear that there have been momentous changes in Ga'dang culture since 1965. In many elements of their culture and associated behavior, modifications as expressed in a loss of culture or an addition to culture are readily apparent. In some cases, the changes have been dramatic, and in others more subtle. The changes range from being mundane—wearing flip-flops instead of going barefoot—to complex—the belief that the Christian God instead of Nanolay is the supreme spiritual being.

Two of the most noticeable changes characterizing Ga'dang villages are their size and their ethnic composition. Prior to 1965, the villages were small, numbering only eight to 12 houses. In many cases, the houses were so scattered throughout the forest that a village was little more than a conglomerate of houses located near slash-and-burn plots, the closer the house was to the uma, the more ideal the situation. By 1965, however, some villages were traditional in size, but a few Ga'dang were turning to plow agriculture, so the houses were constructed closer together, and often, house location reflected kinship.

Today, Ga'dang villages are larger, usually 20 or 25 houses, and, as previously mentioned, constitute a village or a political unit called a sitio, although occasionally the terms purok and sitio are used interchangeably. A Ga'dang purok often is composed of a group of bilateral kin. In the past, houses were built first, and then paths developed between the houses and the swidden fields. Today, a road is constructed and house construction follows.

In 1965, except for trading, the Ga'dang had little interaction with the Ilocano and other ethnic groups in the area. In fact, at that time, there was considerable conflict between the Ga'dang and the Ilocano, as this was a period of rapid Ilocano expansion along the Cordillera Central. The Ga'dang of the time had more interaction with the Balangao speakers from Natonin, but even with these other hill peoples, the relationship was an uneasy one because the Balangao also were competing with the Ga'dang for limited land resources. By the 1980s, the general distrust the Ga'dang had of the Ilocano and other ethnic groups had subsided, and intermarriage between the ethnic groups was becoming more acceptable.

Today, the communities of the Paracelis area are fully mixed with different ethnic groups. The barangay of Bananao is almost 50 percent Ga'dang, followed closely by Balangao, then Ilocano, and then a smattering of other ethnic groups. There is no serious conflict between the Ga'dang and the other ethnic groups in Bananao, although as in many small communities, conflicts do exist between a few individuals.

Villages in 1965 consisted of houses that were similar in size and shape. The houses were generally one-room structures, built on stilts about three or four feet off the ground, the roof was made from cogon thatching, the walls were made from bamboo, and the floor was constructed from split bamboo. There was a hearth in one corner of the house, and the family carried out their household activities in this single structure. Houses were built to last only four or five years because of the need for the Ga'dang to move every few years to a new forest. In 1965, there were only a few Ga'dang tree houses remaining.

Contemporary Ga'dang house structures are built for permanency, they are larger than in the past, and they usually consist of at least two or more rooms. Occasionally they are built on stilts, but more often, they are constructed on the ground. Construction is usually dependent on wealth. The poorer families—usually those with small landholdings—tend to live in the more traditional Ga'dang one-room house. Most Ga'dang families, however, construct their houses from planked boards or cement blocks. They usually have a galvanized roof, two or more rooms, and a kitchen area.

In the barangay of Bananao, most houses have an earthen or cement floor. Very few houses with split bamboo floors exist. The families are equally distributed in the use of propane and fuelwood. The general pattern is a combination of using a small propane stove and a wood-burning hearth. Electricity, rather than bottles filled with kerosene, is available throughout the barangay for lighting.

Some of the most dramatic changes in Ga'dang territory over the past 45 years can be seen in the ecology of the area. In 1965, the forest-covered areas were starting to disappear. Today, except in areas further west into the mountains of the Cordillera Central, the forests are gone. What was in the 1960s a landscape of alternating pockets of forest-cover separated by stretches of grassland is now a sea of cogon grass. The area has been transformed into a specialized ecosystem, dominated by grass and corn. The generalized ecosystem of the past, with its diversity of plant life is limited to the higher elevations of the Cordillera Central. The numerous birds, snakes, spiders, snails, fresh water crab, and the infrequent wild boar, small bands of macaque, and an occasional crocodile are seldom seen, even in the forest. Ga'dang children may know the Ga'dang terms for wild boar or for python, but few of them have ever seen one.

The interdependent relationships between the changing ecosystem and the economic system of the Ga'dang are apparent. Changes in the environment condition the direction the Ga'dang economy takes, and economic activities condition the direction of the environment. The ecosystem is under constant adjustment as the factors of the environment and the economy interact. A change in one system manifests itself in the other system. In the 1965 study, most Ga'dang families built their lives around the rhythm of their slash-and-burn cultivation system. The swidden was a biologically diverse ecosystem where the Ga'dang produced a variety of cultigens for consumption on a daily basis for most of the year. As long as there was a forest in which to create an uma, there were few stimuli for the Ga'dang to change. During the 1965–66 study, the Ga'dang augmented their uma productivity by selling forest products in the lowlands and from fishing and a little hunting. As the forests of the area disappeared, Ga'dang change accelerated.

Because of the change in the environment, sustainability has gone from generalized to specialized. Today, the Ga'dang are dependent on plow farming corn, supplemented by upland rice and a few vegetables produced in their uma. All land in the immediate Bananao area is devoted to growing corn, yielding two crops a year. As corn is labor intensive to grow and process, most Ga'dang corn farmers do not produce a high enough yield to buy rice for the year. Unlike in the past, however, the uma are much smaller and are located one to two hours' walking distance from the village. In order to protect the fertility of the uma land, the Ga'dang now plant only one major crop a year, allowing the land to lie fallow for part of the year.

The change in the environment and the switch to a permanent field crop has dramatically modified the Ga'dang view of land. Although during the 1965–66 study the Ga'dang understood that the forests were disappearing, they perceived land use as a usufruct right. The right to cultivate a particular plot of land was decided by the local Ga'dang. Holding the title to a piece of land was not an issue among the Ga'dang, but today, it is. And, like other Philippine minorities, the Ga'dang are caught in a legal contradiction, which allows them to cultivate public land but prohibits them from cultivating forestland. Ever since the Ga'dang began petitioning for land to title in the 1960s, it has been a quarrelsome issue for the Ga'dang in the Paracelis area, and it remains so today. Since the law requires a surname for titled documents, the Ga'dang have had to abandon their traditional naming system in favor of the one required by the Philippine legal system.

The general features of Ga'dang social organization have changed dramatically since the 1965–66 study. Today, marriages are no longer arranged. The young people take pride in stating that they now have more choice in selecting a spouse, young men speak openly about courting young women, and young women talk about their suitors. There is still a preference for Ga'dang to marry Ga'dang, but this is not a cultural prescription and is becoming less and less important to the Ga'dang. As in the past, sexual liaisons between a young man and a young woman are common and, with pregnancy, often lead to marriage.

In the past, the marriage ceremony was conditioned by the wealth of the parents. Wealthier families killed more pigs, prepared more food, and provided more wine than less wealthy families. Even poor families saved their resources so that they could sponsor at least a small social function for the marriage. Marriage among the Ga'dang is still a social event, but the essential nature of the event is not dependent on the wealth of the family. Today, the wedding ceremony is Christian in orientation, may be performed by a minister or a municipal official, and lasts only an afternoon and evening. All families invite guests, but if the family is wealthy (and there are very few of these families), many guests may be invited. In all cases, the guests will be fed and there may be some modern social dancing in the evening, the music coming from an electrically powered loud speaker. Occasionally, a kiring and lufay may be offered to the girl's family, but since most of the beads and earrings have been sold, the practice today is a rarity. There is very little to distinguish a Ga'dang marriage from the marriage of the Ilocano.

Childbirth still takes place in the home, usually with the aid of a midwife, while in the past, birth was assisted by a local medium, who also served as midwife. Today, the child must be registered with the municipal government at birth, and the child must be registered with a surname. Child-rearing practices of the Ga'dang have changed very little since 1965, except when the child enters elementary school. In the 1965–66 study of Pakak and Cabanuangan, there were no schools for Ga'dang children. Today, the children have the opportunity to attend elementary school and high school; occasionally, a Ga'dang will attend college. When the child enters elementary school, he or she is exposed to children from other ethnic groups on a daily basis, has to learn Ilocano, and is socialized as much at school as at home.

In matters of sociopolitical organization, the Ga'dang presently are just as much a part of the local political structure as any other ethnic group. In the 1965–66 study, the Ga'dang were marginal to the Philippine governmental structure. Today, the Ga'dang at the smallest level of political organization live in a sitio or purok. In the restudy of the Ga'dang, the sitio or purok of Bayongyong is Ga'dang. Other sitio in the area are ethnically mixed. The sitio of Bayongyong is one of several comprising the barangay of Bananao. Bananao is ethnically mixed. Bananao is one barangay of nine, which constitute the municipality of Paracelis, Mountain Province. While the Ga'dang in 1965–66 were subject to Philippine laws, they were not active participants in local politics and were marginal to the governmental system. Today, there are elected Ga'dang officials at the sitio and barangay levels of the political structure, and for the greater municipality, Ga'dang hold important elected and civil positions.

Changes in the spiritual life of the Ga'dang from the 1965–66 study to the present are just as dramatic as the changes in the social, environmental, and economic aspects of Ga'dang life. While some of the Ga'dang still believe or attribute some events to malevolent creatures such as the karangat or the aled, for the most part, misfortune is explained with the Philippine concept of fatalism. Even if an illness might have been caused by a karangat, for example, there are no active female or male mediums, or makamong or mabayen, in Bananao to deal with the illness. With the disappearance of the mediums, the important Ga'dang rites of passage were lost, myths disappeared, the house unting vanished, and the overall spiritual life of the Ga'dang became dominated by Christian beliefs. With the arrival of Christian missionaries, especially the Filipino Pentecostals with their message of "be saved or go to hell," and the translation of the Bible into Ga'dang, Christianity became the dominant belief system of the Ga'dang. By the time of the restudy, the Christian God replaced Nanolay, spirits and germs caused illnesses, treatment of the soul was provided by Christian ministers, and treatment of the body was provided by the local health clinic.

Some of the changes that occurred between the 1965–66 study and the restudy of the Ga'dang are readily apparent—they can be seen, touched, and discussed with Ga'dang individuals. The major stimuli for these changes, however, are broader in scope, interrelated, and less apparent. Nevertheless, they are identifiable. While it would be misleading to order them in degree of importance, some of them may be arranged sequentially.

A major stimulus leading to changes in Ga'dang culture can be traced to the expansion of non-Ga'dang populations into the Cordillera Central. With population growth, especially among Ilocano speakers during the late 1950s and early 1960s, land resources began to decrease rapidly. As Ilocano migrated into the Cagayan Valley and started to stress the environment because of the need to cut more fuelwood for cooking and tobacco drying and the need for farmland, the available land started to disappear, and the migrants began to seek land farther to the west into the Cordillera Central. At the same time, Balangao speakers and Kalinga speakers also needed land and started migrating eastward down the Cordillera Central. The Ga'dang were caught between these two migrant populations, and soon they were forced to look for land to farm elsewhere. Importantly, the forests were disappearing rapidly, so the Ga'dang had to shift dramatically their farming system from slash-and-burn cultivation to plow agriculture. Population increase, the competition for limited land resources, and the destruction of the forests transformed the Cagayan Valley and the eastern slopes of the Cordillera Central into a weed-covered environment. For the Ga'dang, uma cultivation as a primary source of food was no longer possible, and life as a plow farmers would forever change the Ga'dang.

Life for a cultivator who moves every few years in order to find a new forest to farm is markedly different from the life of a permanent field farmer. In the highly fractious and competitive need for farmland, getting title to land became a priority for the Ga'dang. To the good fortune of many of the Ga'dang of the 1965–66 study, they had relatives in the Paracelis area, and land was still available for the Ga'dang to title. This was no easy matter, but once accomplished, living in permanent villages rather in semi-shifting villages brought about significant changes in Ga'dang culture. Different farming techniques, new seeds, the addition of pesticides and fertilizers, modified harvesting techniques, and the processing and the sale of the yields significantly changed the Ga'dang view of economy. In addition, with titled land came taxes, registering with the government, and creating surnames, which caused the Ga'dang to rethink what it was like to be a Ga'dang.

In the early 1970s, the construction of a dirt road was started in the southern part of the Ga'dang area, ending in the northern part of the area at the border with Kalinga. While the road facilitated the arrival of some new materials in the Ga'dang area, it was not until 1983 with the construction of a dam and a bridge at the Magat River that trucks, jeeps, and automobiles were able to move freely between the robust economy of the Cagayan Valley and the mountains of the Ga'dang area. With the bridge, goods, services, and people could move back and forth between the isolated location of Paracelis and the rest of the Philippines in only a matter of hours or a day or so.

Concurrently during the 1970s, Philippine laws were giving an imperfect but higher priority to minorities; schools were built, and health services were becoming available, even if limited, in many rural areas of the Philippines. The Ga'dang took advantage of the opportunities afforded them by the government, especially the new economic and educational opportunities. All of the environmental, economic, educational, and political changes that were affecting the Philippines had a significant impact on Ga'dang culture.

For most Ga'dang, the 45 years between my study of 1965–66 and my restudy was a time of rapid change. Given the conditions of this period, the changes were inevitable, and the Ga'dang accepted them. As an elderly Ga'dang man said to me:

"Napayot kami a Ga'dang." "We Ga'dang are becoming like the others."

Epilogue

T hroughout this book, I have endeavored to be as objective as the discipline of ethnology will permit. Time will be the judge of my success. Now I step from my role as an ethnographer and present a more personal view of change among the Ga'dang. I turn to my more humanistic experiences reflecting my years of fieldwork and address the central question of whether weeds, roads, or God contributed the most to promoting the momentous changes among the Ga'dang described in this book. I have been fortunate to spend at least four months a year, sometimes longer, somewhere in Asia, on two trips a year for the past 33 consecutive years. From the days of my original Ga'dang study, I have been fortunate to witness personally many of the changes described here for the Ga'dang, as well as elsewhere in Asia.

There is no doubt that all three factors contributed to changing the culture and the behavior of the Ga'dang. Importantly, did they contribute equally and in what way did they contribute? For purposes of clarity, I briefly address and speculate on each factor separately.

Now that most of the forest cover on the eastern slopes of the Cordillera Central has been destroyed through illegal logging, slash-and-burn cultivation, fuelwood cutting, agricultural expansion, and overpopulation, as I noted in some of my early publications, the area has become a sea of grass—better yet, a sea of weeds. Once the geneticists discovered, however, that the one commercially viable crop that could compete with cogon grass (with aid from pesticides, fertilizers, and herbicides) was corn, the potential for dramatic environmental change theoretically benefiting the local human population became possible. Today, many areas of the eastern slopes of the Cordillera Central are alternating patches of cornfields separated by fields of cogon grass. Many Ga'dang, especially those families who were quick to claim officially the land their ancestors cultivated, took advantage of corn as a commercial crop. As noted earlier, one Ga'dang man said to me, "We grow corn to buy rice."

What effect did a significantly modified environment and commercial corn growing have on Ga'dang culture? It certainly contributed to changing the Ga'dang economic system from a subsistence slash-and-burn cultivation system to a cash-based system. The behavior associated with farming with a plow became commonplace. Some Ga'dang of the 1960s had already started using the plow. And, of course, most Ga'dang families in Bayongyong still maintain a small slash-and-burn plot in the mountains west of the village. Plow farming led to the Ga'dang living in permanent settlements and a new emphasis being placed on land as inheritance. A permanent place to live significantly contributed to the Ga'dang changing their view of their place in their immediate world. It may have had some impact on reciprocal family labor relationships, but minimally so. The hiring of day laborers has become commonplace. Did growing corn change the fundamental features of Ga'dang social organization? There is nothing to suggest it did, except labor reciprocity is less common than in the past. Did growing corn change the Ga'dang view of their spiritual world? The answer is "No," except that corn may have contributed to the disappearance of the house unting because in earlier times it was taboo to eat corn in the house. While a changing environment and growing corn affected Ga'dang community life, the impact was mainly in the economic sphere of culture. Other changes in Ga'dang culture must be found in roads as a tool of modernization or in the spread of the concept of the Christian God.

There is no doubt that the construction of the dam across the Magat River and the road linking the Ga'dang of the eastern slopes of the Cordillera Central to the commercial centers of the Cagayan Valley had a profound effect on Ga'dang life. In my view, the road, although still mostly unpaved, represents modernization. Before the road, Ga'dang exposure to the outside world was walking up to a week to trade in the Cagayan Valley or meeting with itinerant traders who carried their wares on their backs and hiked from village to village through the mountains. The road exposed Ga'dang communities to government and activity. Government health services and schools were established in the area. The road facilitated this government activity. The road created an opportunity and an awareness that involved the Ga'dang becoming more actively involved in politics. The Ga'dang had votes, and provincial and national politicians could use the road to campaign for these votes. And, of course, there are the more obvious consequences of the road such as jeeps, trucks, buses, and motorcycles. What once could take a week to accomplish could be done in a few hours because of the road. Moreover, within a decade, there was electricity.

The road exposed the Ga'dang to the modern world, but how much did it change their culture? Before the road, building houses with cement blocks would have been unrealistic. Transporting galvanized sheets for granary or house roofs would have been impossible. Transporting the commercial crop of corn to market was very difficult, if not impossible. Frequent contact with the more successful Ilocano (as perceived by the Ga'dang) and the government representatives and merchants of the Poblacion brought more T-shirts, flip-flops, and long pants. Clearly, the many aspects of modernization stimulated profound changes in the lifestyle of the Ga'dang, but did these modern trappings change the core of Ga'dang culture—the worldview and behavior that makes a person "Ga'dang"?

In my view, the road, and its stimulus for governmental intervention and education, is a key factor in the process of changing the core features of Ga'dang culture. Couple the changes brought about by the road with the changes in the environment, and the stage is set for the most powerful change agent to have affected the Ga'dang between my first study and my restudy—God.

I can think of no factor that more dramatically changed Ga'dang core culture—their values and their perception of the world—than the views and conversion techniques promoted by the Christian missionaries, especially the nondenominational and Pentecostal missionaries of the 1960s and 1970s. They were successful in converting most Ga'dang to Christianity. This probably pleases the supporters of the Christian mission field—Ga'dang core beliefs and worldviews have been replaced with Christian beliefs and rituals. For the supporters of cultural pride and ethnic identity, it reflects a stage in the inevitably of modernization, or stated more negatively, it reflects a stage through which minorities become victims of progress.

The Ga'dang, including many children, still speak their own language, but Ilocano is spoken daily in school, by local government officials, and around the community. Most written documents are in Ilocano. Importantly, the Ga'dang vocabulary, especially relative to key cultural concepts, is rapidly disappearing among younger Ga'dang. Rituals associated with naming, rites of passage, marriage, and even burial have all been replaced with Christian beliefs and rituals. Few younger Ga'dang know their history or the mythology associated with their culture. If the younger generation of Ga'dang has ever heard of the culture hero, Nanolay, they know nothing of him except that he is Dios or God. Many Ga'dang accept the Christian view that to practice the solyad is adultery and a sin. "Hell," the "original sin," "salvation through Christ," and "baptism" were meaningless concepts to most the Ga'dang in my original study. Today, such concepts are an everyday part of a generalized Ga'dang worldview.

In brief, except for speaking Ga'dang and claiming an indefinable cultural pride, what is it about the Ga'dang that defines them as a cultural entity and a unique people? My response, simply stated, is—very little.

How the Ga'dang will redefine themselves over the next generation is unclear. If the past is an indication of the future, the Ga'dang will be difficult to recognize as a distinct culture in 50 years. Gone are the traditional clothing, housing, and dances of the Ga'dang except as an expression of cultural pride expressed during community fiestas such as the annual Founders Day event (where young men wear Western underwear under their G-string). Much of their ritual culture has been supplanted with the rituals of Christianity. Government health practitioners now address most of their health issues. The goal in education is for children to attain at least a high school education, and many young people strive to attend provincial colleges. The children are speaking as much Ilocano as they are Ga'dang, and with education, English is rapidly becoming an important language. Many Ga'dang are now active in municipal politics. A few younger Ga'dang have gone abroad to work as domestics in Asia and the Middle East and are sending their families remittances. Others who have worked as domestics are returning to their families with a little money, the latest electrical gadgets, and new ideas. Finally, the cultural homogenizing effects of electricity, cell phones, and television programs should not be underestimated. All of these factors continue to alter Ga'dang culture, but despite these changes, most men and women still perceive themselves as Ga'dang. The idea of being Ga'dang appears less important, however, than being modern Filipino citizens who speak Ga'dang and live in a multicultural environment.

Some Ga'dang believe they are emulating the Ilocano, and probably some of them have this as a goal. In the final analysis, however, the Ga'dang are following the same course of action their immediate ancestors followed and their lowland Christian relatives followed centuries earlier. They are transitioning successfully into the rural cultures of an ever changing and modernizing Philippine nation.

I do not plan to be present in another 50 years to do a restudy of my restudy. This will become the work of another ethnographer. For those ethnographers who might be considering a restudy of earlier research, and it would be good for the profession if some are, know that my restudy of the Ga'dang has been personally and professionally a most rewarding experience. While I, and hopefully my students, have benefited from my research in other areas of Asia, my reintroduction to the Ga'dang has been one of my most personal and rewarding research experiences. Some of this was due to the pleasure of being reunited with old friends and seeing how they have changed. Some of the reward was seeing how Ga'dang culture has evolved. There was also sadness in learning of the death of old friends, and the melancholy of witnessing the disappearance of a rich and vibrant culture. It is not that the novelist Thomas Wolfe was wrong when he said *You Can't Go Home Again* (1934); it is that Wolfe allowed protagonist George Webber to search and find himself, but he did not give Webber the opportunity to redefine himself within the context of the inevitability of change. Perhaps if Wolfe had done this, Webber could have returned home. My journey into the past provided me the opportunity to return home, at least to my professional youth, and the past allowed me to see the present more clearly.

The Origin of the World and the Quarrel between Nanolay and Ofag

(As told by an elderly Ga'dang man from memory in May 1966. Translation by Lidjou Dubadob and the author.)

At a time in the past, the world was made by Nanolay. When it was first made, it was composed of clay and it was spread flat and smooth, like a mat. Nanolay lived here on this flat place, so the water was always flowing. In time, the place where Nanolay lived became flooded, and there was no dry land where he could build his house. Nanolay went to another world . . . somewhere up . . . got some dirt, and brought it back to the flat and wet land. There he put the dirt and built his house.

Once settled on his land, Nanolay first created the rats. The rats lived, and a mother laid her eggs on banana stalks. But, she could not afford to stay long on the banana stalks because it became very hot, and she needed a house in which to live and raise her little rats. Because the mother rat knew where Nanolay had built his house and it was not flooded with water, the mother rat went to Nanolay and asked for a piece of land so she could build a house for her family.

When the mother rat arrived at the house of Nanolay, he said, "What will rats do with a piece of land? Rats do not need land."

The mother rat started to cry, and returned to her children on the banana stalk. She was very sad because Nanolay would not give her a piece of land on which to build a house for her children.

The mother rat returned to the house of Nanolay, and asked again for some dirt on which to build her house. Nanolay took pity on the mother rat and gave her a piece of land that was the size of a guava. Once she received the very small piece of land from Nanolay, she took it in her hands, and patted it and patted it some more until it was large enough for her to build a house for her children.

Unfortunately, the mother rat was not satisfied. She felt that she had not received enough land so she returned to the house of Nanolay and asked for more land. Nanolay refused to give her any more land. Nonetheless, the rat kept returning repeatedly to the house of Nanolay to make the same request for land. Each time she visited Nanolay to make her request, she stuck her fingers in his land. She would stick her fingers in the land every time she went to see Nanolay. Therefore, after each trip to visit the house of Nanolay, the mother rat was able to carry back some dirt from the land of Nanolay to her own house. As time passed, the land of the mother rat became larger and larger. Each time she returned from the house of Nanolay, she added dirt to the land. When she had no work to do, she would spend her time patting the dirt between her hands, and soon her land became the earth. The land became big with high mountains and flat places. It became dufafa . . . earth.

When Nanolay saw that the work of the rat was completed, he said to her, "Rat . . . you see what you have done? You have completed your work but you have done it by stealing my ground."

"Oh . . . no, Nanolay," the rat replied. "What you see is the ground that you have given me. The ground stuck to my hand when I was coming to your house. This is my work. I have not stolen your ground."

Nanolay believed what the rat had told him. He was pleased with the work of the mother rat. He was happy that she had made the mountains and she had made the flatland.

Nanolay, however, thought to himself, "This land is of no use if I do not make a man to live on it. I will make a *lalaki*."

Nanolay made a man and this man lived on the earth. But, the man was very unhappy because he was always accompanied by rats. He could have no children by himself or with a rat. In time, Nanolay decided that there should be a pair of humans. He knew it was not possible to produce children without a pair. As the man slept, Nanolay came and took a bone from the body of the man. He placed the bone behind the man as he slept. When the man woke, he discovered there was a woman behind him. Because the woman that man had found behind him was beautiful, he decided they should produce children and they did. Their children produced children, and their children produced children, and they were the descendants of the first man and woman.

After Nanolay had watched these human beings produce many children, and then more children, Nanolay became so happy with what he had done that he wanted to marry one of these human beings. He saw a beautiful woman and she agreed to marry him. The name of Nanolay's wife was Bilokan. Bilokan was the only daughter of the family, but she had two brothers, Sabukal and Isik. Nanolay, Bilokan, Sabukal, and Isik all moved to earth.

After Nanolay and Bilokan were settled on earth, his cousin Ofag came to join them. The sisters of Nanolay also came down to earth. The oldest sister was Kwamat, and the other sisters were named Burak, Menalam, and Sambabayan.

The parents of Nanolay called down from kalekay and shouted, "Nanolay . . . you will have nothing to do unless you produce children." So, Nanolay and Bilokan decided to have children on earth where they had moved.

When Bilokan was pregnant, Nanolay said to her, "Wait my wife, I must first go to kalekay."

As Nanolay was getting ready to leave for kalekay, he said to his wife, "Tell your brothers they are not to touch my wine. I will go to kalekay, and when I return, we will make an among. We will make a feast."

While Nanolay was in kalekay, the brothers of Bilokan came to the house, and they were very proud and boastful men.

Bilokan said, "Do not touch the wine of Nanolay. We have something to do with the wine."

But the brothers of Bilokan did not obey her, and they drank and they drank the wine that Nanolay had said that they were not to drink. They drank and drank, but it was an endless supply of wine. They drank so much wine that they became very drunk.

The brothers said in anger, "What kind of wine is this? There is no end to this wine." The brothers were drunk and they became angry. They threw the wine jar against a post and the neck of the wine jar broke. When the wine jar broke, the wine flowed like water in a stream.

When Nanolay returned from kalekay to the earth, he was accompanied by his brothers. He had invited them to come with him because he was planning an *unting* [in this case a ritual] or an occasion. But, because the wine was gone, he could not hold the feast.

The brother of Nanolay said to him, "There is nothing we can do. The wine is gone. We will have to have the unting at another time."

Nanolay responded in anger, "How can I see my people happy if we cannot have a feast? The people need to have a feast."

Nanolay became so angry that he started killing birds, lizards, and all animals. He killed all kinds of animals. After killing them, he took them to his house. When he got to the house, he started shouting and beat his gong. But, only he could hear the sounds of the gong.

Still angry, Nanolay shouted, "I have killed all kinds of animals. It is only a human being that I have not killed. I will kill a human being. I will kill one so that my descendents will be happy and proud of me."

Nanolay killed the son of his cousin Ofag. After killing the son of Ofag, he ran home shouting that he had killed the son of Ofag, and he shouted so loud that the whole earth heard his shouting. He beat his gong, and he beat his gong some more, so that the sound of the gong could be heard in all places.

Nanolay then shouted in joy to the world, "It is good that human beings can kill each other. The gongs could be heard in all places. I will have a feast in celebration. It is an honor to celebrate."

All who wanted came to the occasion. They drank wine, they ate pig, and they danced with the gong. Ofag was the only person who did not come to the occasion. He was sorry that Nanolay had killed his son.

Ofag did not bury the son that was killed by Nanolay because it was his wish that his son would be alive again. Nanolay, however, did not want the son of Ofag to live again.

Nanolay said, "If I allow the son of Ofag to live again, then all people that are killed must also live again."

But Nanolay deceived Ofag. Because Ofag was unhappy, Nanolay pretended to let the son of Ofag live again. The body of Ofag's son had already turned to bone. So, Nanolay covered the bones with a woven blanket, and when he removed the blanket, the bones turned into a human being. When Nanolay covered the body with the blanket again, it returned to bones.

Ofag was very angry over what Nanolay had done. Ofag knew that Nanolay could have allowed his son to return to life, but Nanolay refused to do it. Ofag became so angry that he tried to kill Nanolay. But Nanolay was able to jump away and run to his house. Ofag chased him with a spear and a machete, but because Nanolay had the will of *makapangwa* [all power], Ofag was not able to kill him. Nanolay was so upset over Ofag trying to kill him, he could not eat, and he could not work. Even though Nanolay had the makapangwa, he did not want to use it against Ofag.

Nanolay said to Ofag, "Wait, I will give you a kiring."

Ofag refused the kiring and shouted at Nanolay, "I will kill you Nanolay!"

"If you kill me, you will kill me," Nanolay replied. "If you cannot kill me you cannot kill me."

Nanolay then offered Ofag all of his wealth, but Ofag refused it. Ofag remained so angry that he burned the house of Nanolay.

Because Nanolay could not eat because of Ofag always trying to kill him, he went to *Adug* [thunder] and *Talit* [lightening], told them what Ofag was doing to him, and asked them to intervene with Ofag.

Adug and Talit immediately asked, "We understand, but what kind of bead have you offered Ofag?"

"I have offered him a kiring, some gold, and all my wealth but he refuses to take it."

Adug and Talit agreed to represent Nanolay and said, "You give us two pieces of the *galdak* (a rare bead)."

Adug and Talit went to Ofag carrying the offering from Nanolay, but Ofag would not accept the offering. This made Adug and Talit very angry, so they began making so much noise and causing so much rain.

Ofag was very frightened, and he shouted, "Even if you kill me, I will not accept the galdak!"

In time, Ofag was afraid for his life, so he accepted the galdak, and he told all that he was forced to accept the offering.

One day, Ofag went to the house of Nanolay and said, "Nanaloy, what you have done to my son is something that your descendents will suffer for, and their descendents will suffer for, and their descendents will suffer for. You have given a wrong, and this wrong will be the suffering of your descendents."

The Two Orphans
and the Karangat

*(As told by an elderly Ga'dang man from memory in June 1966.
Translation by Lidjou Dubadob and the author.)*

At the time of the first people, there were two young orphan girls. They decided to go out one day and pick some beans. While picking the beans, they found a small baby under the leaves of the beans. The baby was laughing at them while they picked the beans. The orphans looked carefully at the baby and saw that he had only two teeth. The teeth were very unusual because they were long, and they were sharp, and they curved out from the lips. These two orphans decided to bring the baby home. They were happy because they had a baby.

The orphans said, "We are happy. We have a baby."

What the two orphans did was to feed the baby very much, and to love the baby because they wanted him to grow strong. After one year of caring for the baby, the two orphans found out that the baby had grown and had already learned how to cook gruel. His sharp teeth were lost so he had to eat gruel.

Because the baby could already cook his own food, the orphans said to him, "Remain home and we will go and work and find some rice for you to cook."

Every afternoon when the orphans retuned home from their work, they found that the baby had prepared stacks of wood for fuel for the fire. The wood was chopped in to small pieces. They did this ten times and each time they returned home, they found that the baby had prepared wood for the fire. The orphans were very surprised that a baby could do this kind of work. They made an agreement with each other to watch and see how the baby was able to do this work.

So, one day, they pretended to the baby that they were going to work in the uma, but they did not go to work. They hid and watched the baby. What the baby did was take his two large teeth from a bamboo tube where he had hidden them earlier. After the orphans were gone, he took his two large teeth and used them in chopping the trees. When he put his teeth in his mouth, he became a fully-grown man. His teeth were now very long. The two sisters saw him cut down the big tree and then chop it into sticks for fuelwood with his teeth. After he finished chopping the wood, he removed his two teeth from his mouth and hid them again in the bamboo tubes. When he did this, he returned to being a baby.

The baby said to himself, "I will not let them see that I become a man and then return to a baby. I will wait, and when the two sisters grow bigger, I will eat them."

The orphans became frightened of what they had seen, so they ran away. They went into the forest. When they reached the forest, they found a lime tree. The two orphans climbed high into the tree and they became the fruit of the tree. They were fruit at the very top branches.

One sister said to the other, "Don't make any noise my sister. We do not want the karangat to know we are here. We are afraid to be eaten by the karangat."

That afternoon when the two sisters did not return home, the baby was surprised. They had never failed to return home before. The baby was eager to find them. He smelled to the north, to the east, to the west, and the south. He discovered that they had fled north. He knew this because of the human smell they had left behind. The baby followed the human smell. Finally, he reached the lime tree where the sisters had hidden by becoming fruit of the lime. When he reached the lime tree, and he smelled that the fruit had a human being smell, he was karangat.

He said loudly, "I will eat all of the fruit on the lime tree."

When the karangat had eaten most of the fruit on the tree, the sisters became worried because they were afraid they would soon be eaten. Out of fear, they fell to the ground, and rolled and rolled down the hill. After a long distance, the two sisters once again turned into human beings. They ran further into the forest looking for a place to hide. Soon, they found a wild guava tree and climbed it. There they hid by turning themselves into the fruit of the wild guava, again hanging from the very top branches.

At the lime tree, the karangat was angry. He knew the sisters had run away, but he was hungry. He said to himself, "First, I will eat all the fruit on this tree, and then I will find the sisters. I will eat them."

After the karangat had eaten all the fruit on the lime tree, he started tracing the smell of the sisters. He walked through the forest until he found a guava tree that smelled of humans.

He said, "I will eat all the fruit that is on this guava tree."

But, as the guava tree was near the bank of a stream, the sisters told one another, "We will fall down my sister and we will become fish. The karangat will not know where we are because we will be in the water."

The two sisters then fell from the tree into the water and they became fish.

Realizing what the orphans had done, the karangat shouted, "Go ahead and run away. First I will eat all the fruit on this guava tree. Then I will look and find you. I will find you and I will eat you."

After eating all the fruit on the guava tree, the karangat jumped into the stream and began catching fish and eating them. He did this because he knew if he ate enough fish, he would soon find the two sisters. When the orphans learned that almost all the fish in the stream had been eaten by the karangat, they started swimming north. They swam very far. When they thought they had escaped, they changed again to human beings. And, again, they ran away.

While running along a path near a village they saw a handsome young man preparing betel nut and lime. The young man was very surprised to see two young women running along the path.

"Why are you two you women running along the path?" he asked. "It seems that you are very frightened."

One of the orphans replied, "Young gentleman, don't bother us. Karangat is chasing us. We must run. You must be careful because if he sees you, he will eat you."

"Rest first," he said. "We will chew some betel. I do not think the karangat is following you."

The young man wanted very much to introduce himself to the young women. He thought that they were the most beautiful girls he had ever seen, so he said, "My name is Wigan. What is your name?"

He learned from the orphans that the older girl was named Bagiamuk, and the younger sister was named Anus.

The young man said to the sisters, "Go inside our house. Don't worry, nothing will happen to you. I will stay here and wait for the karangat."

The two sisters replied, "We must leave you. We do not want you to be bothered with us. It is dangerous to you to wait for the karangat."

"Go into our house," he answered. "I will wait for the karangat and I will fight him. If he defeats me, it is all right to me. If I defeat him, it is good that we all may live."

The sisters agreed with the young man, and they went into the house. As soon as they had entered the house, the karangat appeared in the place where the young man was preparing his betel nut and lime.

The karangat said to the young man, "You are very smelly. You smell like a human being."

The young man answered, "Karangat, if you do not touch me, I will tell you something that you want to know. If you touch me, there is nothing that I can teach you. If you don't touch me, I will tell you where to find what you are looking for."

"All right," the karangat replied. "That is a good idea you have. I want to find them and eat them. I am very tired."

"Yes," said the young man. "But there is one condition. Let us first chew betel. I will then teach you what you want to know."

"Agreed," replied the karangat.

The young man said to the karangat, "Open your mouth and close your eyes."

When the karangat opened his mouth and closed his eyes, the young man took five betel nut, five small bundles of *ikmu* leaves, and two bamboo tubes of lime, and attacked the karangat. The young man stuffed the betel nut and the *ikmu* leaves in the mouth of the karangat. The young man then started pouring the lime in the mouth, eyes, and the nose of the karangat. The karangat became very angry. He started reaching and reaching for the young man, but he could not see because of the lime in his eyes.

The karangat shouted, "If I had known that is what you were going to do to me, I would have eaten you as soon as I arrived here."

"This is your fate," the young man replied. "This is your fate, and what you deserve because of what you want to do to the young sisters."

Because the karangat was blinded by the lime in his eyes, he began feeling about frantically trying to find his way to the stream. He finally reached the stream, but the young man followed him. When the karangat reached the stream, he washed his face. When the water reached his face, it mixed with the lime, and it started to boil in his eyes and in his mouth and in his nose. Soon, there was so much boiling of the water that the karangat died.

After the karangat died, the young man returned to his parents' house and found the two sisters. The parents of the young man were very happy because the young man was their only son and he had met two sisters.

The parents said to their son, "These two young women came to you, and you helped them escape the karangat. If you want, select one of them and you will be married."

He answered, "If they like me, and you like them, I will marry one of them."

The mother said to her son, "Which one of the young women do you like?"

"I will marry both of them," he replied.

After some long discussion, the sisters said, "Be patient with us. No one will feed us because we are orphans."

"Never mind," the parents of the young man said. "You two sisters will be the ones to marry our son."

"Does he agree that both of us will be his wife?" the sisters asked.

"Yes," replied the parents of the young man. "We are agreed that both of you will be his wife. Change your clothes."

After changing their clothes, the two young sisters became even more beautiful than they were before. In a few days, they celebrated the wedding, and it was a joyful event because many people attended the occasion.

Glossary

abag   G-string
abat   banana
abok   hair on top of head
abut na iyung   hole in nose
afu   grandparents/grandchildren
agagwa   ritual purification of new house
alat   talisman to protect a household
aled   transubstantial malevolent spirit
alifangbang   butterfly
ama   father
among   one of the most important rituals
anak   child
angakokang   invisible malevolent spirit
anitu   general linguistic gloss for spiritual power
antolay   carved wooden household talisman
apai   rice
aran   malevolent spirit that appears as mist
arawarawi   pole around which to dance
atawa   spouse
atong   jaw teeth
atu   dog
bafui   domesticated pig
bafui natatun   wild boar
baginatnat   headdress of rattan worn by a female medium
bakao   corn
balinsioa   eggplant
balog   rite of passage ritual for a child
balu   widow
balug   dove

baowi   small hut for shifting cultivation observation; house where a dead person rests

barangay   native Filipino term for a village, district, or ward

biki   complete skull

bingil   physically distorted humanlike ghoul

bu'lao   neck area of body

bulatung   mungo beans

burasi   carp

busing   selecting and cutting a shifting cultivation site

dafug   carabao

dalamit   temple of skull

dalug   mudfish

damuan   front teeth

dangu   onion

dapan   complete foot

darara   shed for sitting

daruru   back of body

dinat   maya bird

dufafa   earth world

gurok   green pigeon

galating   musical instrument made from bamboo

gasilung   camote

gitalun   wild chicken

gured   scabies/skin disease

ikit   aunt

ilosa   world of the past and the present

ilug   chicken egg

iming   chin or cheek hair

ina   mother

incanto   malevolent magic

kabirat   spouse's sibling's spouse

kafalay   child's spouse's parents

kalekay   up-after world

kamaran   wealthy family

kamat   complete hand

kapingsan   cousin

kararawa   soul of a dead creature

katawangan   spouse's parents, spouse's parents' siblings

kimat   eyebrows and/or eye lashes

kiri   forehead

kolak   sibling; friend

kubang   talisman to protect a household

kukirao   sharkfish

kuliwag   small talisman for a house

kurawit   ritual for new household

ladao   fresh water shrimp

lalaki   male

lamag   crocodile

langalay   complete arm

layag   complete nose

lufay   valuable set of bead earrings

lupon   local Philippine dispute mediator council

luton   one of several house talismans

lutong   wood and rattan house talisman

mabayen   male medium

mabini   planting rice or corn

mabuwat   harvesting the field

madot   tying shifting cultivation rice in bundles

mafuyat   midwife

magani   harvesting rice or corn

maganu   drying the shifting cultivation site

magatu   harvesting tobacco

makadwa   major rite of passage ritual

maka'lu   important adult rite of passage

makamel   cleaning the shifting cultivation site

makamong   female medium

makat   reburning shifting cultivation site

malamun   weeding the field

malandak   pulling weeds from the shifting cultivation site

mamilag   drying rice

mamula   planting the field/planting vegetables

mamuwawan   protecting the field

manuk   chicken

manuwang   spouses of sons and daughters

maparagut   harrowing the field

maradu   plowing

mata   complete eye

matabas   cleaning the field for plowing

mataraw   trimming the trees

mimunaw   a rice-planting rite

miudu   storing rice in a granary

nana   millet

Nanolay   cultural hero and creator of world

napayot   to become like

nauma   shifting cultivation site is cut

Ofag   cousin of *Nanolay*

paiyan   crawfish

palatao   machete

panganakan   children of siblings and cousins

pangit   widower

paniki   fruit bat
papa   wild duck
paringel   upper and lower lips
patat   catfish
patung   hip area of body
pidwana busing   second cutting of shifting cultivation site
pisel   marriage ceremony
Poblacion   central *barangay* of a Philippine municipality
pudon   peace-pact system
purok   subdivision of a Philippine *barangay*
sari-sari   small local variety store
sayay   betel nut bag
sikulan   burning field debris
sillay   general term for beads
singafui   camote leaves
sitio   village
solyad   spouse exchange
sukulan   burning debris in shifting cultivation site
ta'gang   chest
talun   forests
tantel   back of head
tolay   humans or people
tuwan   partner in certain rituals
ule   complete head
ulitag   uncle
uma   slash-and-burn plot
unting   ritual house-items protecting a house
urung   snail
uta   deer
utak   brain
uwao   monkey
waiyi   relative
wangit   complete mouth

References

Aduarte, Diego. 1640. "Historia de la Provincia del Santo Rosario Orden de Predica-dores," vol. 30–32, in *The Philippine Islands* (E. Blair and J. A. Robertson, eds.). Cleveland: A.H. Clark.

Amselle, Jean-Loup. 2002. "Globalization and the Future of Anthropology." *African Affairs* 101(403):213–229.

Anderson, Allan and Edmond Tang, eds. 2005. *Asian and Pentecostal: The Charismatic Face of Christianity in Asia.* Oxford, UK, and Baguio City, Philippines: Regnum Books International and APTS Press.

Bagyan, Fernando, and Lulu Gimenez. 2005. "Corn Farming in Alfonso Lista." *Bulatlat.* 5(38). http://www.bulatlat.com/news/5-38/5-38-corn.htm.

Bananao Census. 2010. *Official Census of Bananao, 2010.* Bananao: Recorded by the Secretary of the Barangay.

Barth, Fredrik. 1967. "On the Study of Social Change." *American Anthropologist* 69(6):661–669.

Barton, Roy F. 1919. "Ifugao Law." *University of California Publications in American Archaeology and Ethnology* 15(1):1–127. http://digitalassets.lib.berkeley.edu/anthpubs/ucb/text/ucp015-003.pdf.

———. 1938. *Philippine Pagans: The Autobiographies of Three Ifugaos.* London: George Rutledge and Sons, Ltd.

———. 1946. "The Religion of the Ifugaos." *Memoirs of the American Anthropological Association* 65:1–219.

———. 1949. *The Kalingas.* Chicago: The University of Chicago Press.

Beatty, Andrew. 2010. "How Did It Feel for You? Emotion, Narrative, and the Limits of Ethnography." *American Anthropologist* 12(3):430–443.

Bentley, Michael. 1999. *Modern Historiography: An Introduction.* London: Routledge.

Benedict, Ruth. 1934. *Patterns of Culture.* Boston and New York: Houghton, Mifflin.

Berreman, Gerald. 1966. Anemic and Emetic Analysis in Social Anthropology. *American Anthropologist* 68(2):346–354.

Beyer, H. Otley. 1917. *Population of the Philippine Islands in 1916.* Manila: Philippine Education Co.

———. 1953. Address of Professor H. Otley Beyer as presiding officer at the opening session of the Fourth Far-Eastern Prehistory Congress, Nov. 16. Manila.

Bible League. 2000. *Ino Sapiti Dios: Bawuwa Tulag.* Manila: The Bible League, the Philippine Bible Society.

Blair, Emma Helen, and James Alexander Robertson. 1907. "Augustinian Parishes and Missions, 1760." In *The Philippine Islands: 1751–1765,* Vol. 48. Emma Helen Blair and James Alexander Robertson, eds. Cleveland: A. H. Clark.

Boas, Franz. 1888. *The Central Eskimo.* Washington, DC: Bureau of Ethnology, Smithsonian Institution.

Bohannan, Laura (pen name Elenore Smith Bowen). 1954. *Return to Laughter: An Anthropological Novel.* London: Victor Gollancz.

Bruner, Edward M. 1986. "Ethnography as Narrative." In *The Anthropology of Experience.* Victor W. Turner and Edward M. Bruner, eds. Pp. 139–158. Urbana and Chicago: University of Illinois Press.

Burling, Robbins. 1964. "Cognition and Componential Analysis: God's Truth or Hocus-Pocus?" *American Anthropologist* 66(1):20–28.

CAR. 2010. "Paracelis." National Economic Research and Business Assistance Center, http://www.nerbac-car.ph/mt-province/Paracelis.html.

Chagnon, Napoleon A. 1968. *Yanomanö: The Fierce People.* New York: Holt, Rinehart and Winston.

Chapman, K. G. 1962. *Icelandic–Norwegian Linguistic Relationships.* Oslo: Universitetsforlaget.

Chicago. 2009. Guide to the University of Chicago Philippines Studies Program Records. University of Chicago Library. http://www.lib.uchicago.edu/e/scrc/findingaids/view.php.

Chick, Garry. 2000. "Writing Culture Reliably: The Analysis of High-Concordance Codes." *Ethnology* 39(4):365–393.

Chikoye, D., V. M. Manyong, R. Carsky, F. Ekeleme, G. Gbehounou, and A. Ahanchede. 2002."Response of Speargrass (*Imperata cylindrica*) to Cover Crops Integrated with Hand-Weeding and Chemical Control in Maize and Cassava." *Crop Protection* 21:145–156.

Conklin, Harold C. 1957. *Hanunoo Agriculture in the Philippines: A Report on the Integral System of Shifting Cultivation in the Philippines.* Rome: FAO Food and Agriculture Organization of the United Nations.

———. 1980. *Ethnographic Atlas of Ifugao: A Study of Environment, Culture, and Society in Northern Luzon.* New York: American Geographical Society of New York.

Cole, Fay-Cooper. 1915. *Traditions of the Tinguian: A Study in Philippine Folk-Lore.* Chicago: Field Museum Natural History Publication 180.

Crisologo-Mendoza, Lorelei, and June Prill-Brett. 2009. "Communal Land Management in the Cordillera Region of the Philippines." In *Land and Cultural Survival: The Communal Land Rights of Indigenous Peoples in Asia.* Jayantha Perera, ed. Pp. 38–61. Mandaluyong City: Asian Development Bank.

Davies, Charlotte A. 1999. *Reflexive Ethnography: A Guide to Researching Selves and Others.* New York: Routledge.

Dozier, Edward P. 1966. *Mountain Arbiters: The Changing Life of a Philippine Hill People.* Tucson: The University of Arizona Press.

———. 1967. *The Kalinga of Northern Luzon, Philippines.* New York: Holt, Rinehart and Winston.

Dyen, Isidore. 1975. *Linguistic Subgrouping and Lexicostatistics.* The Hague: Mouton.

Edelman, Marc, and Angelique Haugerud, eds. 2005. *The Anthropology of Development and Globalization: From Classical Political Economy to Contemporary Neoliberalism.* Blackwell Anthologies in Social and Cultural Anthropology. Malden, MA: Blackwell.

Eder, James F. 1987. *On The Road to Tribal Extinction: Depopulation, Deculturation, and Adaptive Well-Being*. Berkeley: University of California Press.

Eriksen, Thomas Hylland, ed. 2003. *Globalization: Studies in Anthropology*. London: Pluto Press.

————. 2007. *Globalization: The Key Concepts*. Oxford: Berg.

Eggan, Fred. 1960. "The Sagada Igorots of Northern Luzon." In *Social Structure in Southeast Asia*. G. P. Murdock, ed. New York: Wenner-Gren Foundation for Anthropological Research.

————. 1963. "Fay-Cooper Cole, 1881–1961." *American Anthropologist* 65(3):641–648.

Executive Order. 1987. The Family Code of the Philippines, Executive Order No. 209. www.chanrobles.com/executiveorderno209.htm.

Firth, Raymond. 1959. *Social Change in Tikopia: Re-study of a Polynesian Community after a Generation*. London: Allen and Unwin.

Foster, George M., Thayer Scudder, Elizabeth Colson, and Robert V. Kemper, eds. 1979. *Long-Term Field Research in Anthropology*. New York: Academic Press.

Fox, Robert B. 1953. "The Pinatubo Negritos: Their Useful Plants and Material Culture." *The Philippine Journal of Science* 81:3–4.

Fox, Jefferson, Yayoi Fujita, Dimbab Ngidang, Nancy Peluso, Lesley Potter, Niken Sakuntaladewi, Janet Sturgeon, and David Thomas. 2009. "Policies, Political-Economy, and Swidden in Southeast Asia." *Human Ecology* 37(3):305–322.

Frake, Charles O. 1964a. "How to Ask for a Drink in Subanun." *American Anthropologist* 66(6):127–132.

————. 1964b. "Notes on Queries in Ethnology." *American Anthropologist* 66(3):99–131.

Freeman, J. Derek. 1955. *Iban Agriculture: A Report on the Shifting Cultivation of Hill Rice by the Iban of Sarawak*. London: Her Majesty's Stationery Office.

————. 1983. *Margaret Mead and Samoa: The Making and Unmaking of an Anthropological Myth*. Boston: Harvard University Press.

Fujisaka, S., P. Sajise, and R. del Castillo, eds. 1986. *Man, Agriculture and the Tropical Forest: Change and Development in the Philippine Islands*. Bangkok: Winrock International Institute for Agriculture Development.

Gaillard, J. C., and J. P. Mallari. 2004. "The Peopling of the Philippines: A Cartographic Synthesis." *Journal of the University of the Philippines Archaeological Studies Program* 6:1–27.

Galang, Ricardo E. 1935. "Ethnographic Study of the Yogads of Isabela." *Philippine Journal of Science* 56(1):81–94.

Gatbonton, Juan T. 2010. "Dropouts: Our Immense and Invisible Failure." *Manila Times*, June 6, editorial page.

Geddes, William R. 1954. *The Land Dayaks of Sarawak*. London: Her Majesty's Stationery Office.

————. 1985. "Review of: *Ethnographic Atlas of Ifugao*, by Harold C. Conklin." *Oceania* 55(4):309–310.

Geertz, Clifford. 1973. *The Interpretation of Cultures*. New York: Basic Books.

GISD. 2010. *Imperata cylindrica*, Global Invasive Species Database. http://www.issg.org/database/species/ecology.

Goodenough, Ward H. 1956. "Componential Analysis and the Study of Meaning." *Language* 32(1):195–216.

Guyer, Jane I. 1997. *An African Niche Economy: Farming to Feed Ibadan, 1968–88*. Edinburgh: Edinburgh University Press.

Halstead, Narmala, Eric Hirsch, and Judith Okely, eds. 2008. *Knowing How to Know: Fieldwork and the Ethnographic Present*. Oxford: Berghahn Books.

Harris, Marvin. 1979. *Cultural Materialism: The Struggle for a Science of Culture.* New York: Random House.

Hart, Gillian. 2004. *Power, Labor, and Livelihood: Processes of Change in Rural Java: Notes and Reflections on a Village Revisited.* Berkeley: University of California Press.

Heaney, Lawrence R. 1998. "The Causes and Effects of Deforestation." In *Vanishing Treasures of the Philippines Rain Forest.* J. C. Regalado, Jr. and L. R. Heaney, eds. Pp. 61–67. Chicago: The Field Museum.

Holmes, Lowell D. 1987. *Quest for the Real Samoa: The Mead/Freeman Controversy and Beyond.* South Hadley, MA: Bergin and Garvey.

Honigman, John J. 1963. *Kaska Indians: An Ethnographic Reconstruction.* New Haven, CT: Yale University Publications in Anthropology no. 51.

Hoskins, Janet, ed. 1996. *Headhunting and the Social Imagination in Southeast Asia.* Palo Alto, CA: Stanford University Press.

Huke, Robert E. 1963. *Shadows on the Land: An Economic Geography of the Philippines.* Makati, Philippines: Carmelo and Bauermann.

Hymes, Dell 1960. "Lexicostatistics So Far." *Current Anthropology* 1(1):3–44.

Inda, Jonathan Xavier, and Renato Rosaldo, eds. 2007. *The Anthropology of Globalization: A Reader.* Oxford: Blackwell.

Jaarsma, S. R., and Marta Rohatynskyj, eds. 2000. *Ethnographic Artifacts: Challenges to a Reflexive Anthropology.* Honolulu: University of Hawai'i Press.

Jenkins, Keith, ed. 1997. *The Postmodern History Reader.* London: Routledge.

Jenks, A. Ernest. 1905. *The Bontoc Igorot.* Philippine Ethnological Survey Publications. Manila: Bureau of Public Printing. Online Reader: www.gutenberg.org/catalog/world/readfile?fk_files=1451871.

Jocano, F. Landa. 1975. *Philippine Prehistory: An Anthropological Overview of the Beginnings of Filipino Society and Culture.* Dilman: Philippine Center for Advanced Studies, University of the Philippines system.

Jolly, Margaret. 1992. "Banana Leaf Bundles and Skirts: A Pacific Penelope's Web?" In *History and Tradition in Melanesian Anthropology.* James C. Carrier, ed. Pp. 38–64. Berkeley, Los Angeles, Oxford: University of California Press.

Jones, William. 1907–1909. *The Diary of William Jones: 1907–1909, Robert F. Cummings Philippine Expedition.* Dumbato, Isabela Province, Luzon, Philippines: The Field Museum of Chicago.

Kay, Paul, and Willett Kempton. 1984. "What Is the Sapir-Whorf Hypothesis?" *American Anthropologist* 86(1):65–79.

Keesing, Felix M. 1962. *The Ethnohistory of Northern Luzon.* Palo Alto, CA: Stanford University Press.

Kehoe, Alice B., et al. 2010. "Return to the Natives." Presentation of the Association of Senior Anthropologists. 109th Annual Meeting, American Anthropological Association, New Orleans, Session 2-0240.

Kemper, Robert V., and Anya Peterson Royce, eds. 2002. *Chronicling Cultures: Long-Term Field Research in Anthropology.* Walnut Creek, CA: Altamira Press.

Knauft, Bruce M. 2002. *Exchanging the Past: A Rainforest World of Before and After.* Chicago: University of Chicago Press.

Kroeber, Alfred L. 1948. *Anthropology.* New York: Harcourt, Brace & Worlds.

———. 1949. "Roy Franklin Barton, 1883–1947." *American Anthropologist* 51(1):91–95.

Kummer, David M. 1991. *Deforestation in the Postwar Philippines.* Chicago: University of Chicago Press.

Lambrecht, Godfrey. 1959. "The Gaddang of Isabela and Nueva Vizcaya: Survivals of a Primitive Animistic Religion." *Philippines Studies* 7:194–218.

———. 1960. "Anitu Rites Among the Gaddang." *Philippine Studies* 8:584–602.

Landor, A. Henry Savage. 1904. *The Gems of the East*. New York: Harper and Brothers.

Lett, James W. 1997. *Science, Reason, and Anthropology: The Principles of Rational Inquiry*. Oxford: Rowman & Littlefield.

Lewis, Oscar. 1951. *Life in a Mexican Village: Tepotzlan Restudied*. Urbana: University of Illinois Press.

Lewis, Paul M., ed. 2009. *Ethnologue: Languages of the World*. Dallas: SIL International.

Lewellen, Ted C. 2002. *The Anthropology of Globalization: Cultural Anthropology Enters the 21st Century*. Westport, CT: Bergin and Garvey.

Lieban, Richard W. 1966. "Fatalism and Medicine in Cebuano Areas of the Philippines." *Anthropological Quarterly* 39(3):171–179.

Linde, Charlotte. 1993. *Life Stories: The Creation of Coherence*. New York: Oxford University Press.

Lucy, John A. 1997. "Linguistic Relativity." *Annual Review of Anthropology* 26:291–312.

Lumicao-Lormaa, Maria Luisa. 1984. *Gaddang Literature*. Quezon City, Philippines: New Day.

Lumahan, Cornado. 2005. "Facts and Figures: A History of the Growth of the Philippine Assemblies of God." *American Journal of Political Science* 8(2):331–344.

MacDonald, G. E. 2004. "Cogon Grass (*Imperata cylindrica*)—Biology, Ecology, and Management." *Critical Reviews in Plant Science* 23:367–380.

Malinowski, Bronislaw. 1984[1922]. *Argonauts of the Western Pacific*. Long Grove, IL: Waveland Press.

Malumbres, Julian. 1918. *Historia de la Isabela*. Manila: Santo Thomas University.

Mangahas, Mahar. 2010. "The Institute of Philippine Culture, at 50." *Philippine Daily Inquirer*.

Mead, Margaret. 1928. *Coming of Age in Samoa: A Psychological Study of Primitive Youth for Western Civilization*. New York: William Morrow.

Murdock, George P. 1934. *Our Primitive Contemporaries*. New York: Macmillan.

Nader, Laura. 1970. "Review of Reissue of *Ifugao Law* by Roy F. Barton." Berkeley and Los Angeles: University of California Press.

NCCR (National Conference on Cordillera Researches). 2000. *Towards Understanding Peoples of the Cordillera: A Review of Research on History, Governance, Resources, Institutions, and Living Traditions*. Baguio: University of the Philippines, Cordillera Studies Center.

Ng, Judy. 2007. *Harold C. Conklin Philippine Collection*. Washington, DC: American Folklife Center, Library of Congress.

Ochs, Elinor, and Lisa Capps. 1996. "Narrating the Self." *Annual Review of Anthropology* 25:19–43.

Orans, Martin. 1996. *Not Even Wrong: Margaret Mead, Derek Freeman, and the Samoans*. Novato, CA: Chandler and Sharp.

Ortner, Sherry B. 1984. "Theory in Anthropology since the Sixties." *Comparative Studies in Society and History* 26(1):126–166.

Peacock, James L., and Dorothy C. Holland. 1993. "The Narrated Self: Life Stories in Process." *Ethos* 24(4):367–383.

Perry, Richard J. 1983. "Proto-Athapaskan Culture: The Uses of Ethnographic Reconstruction." *American Ethnologist* 10(4):715–733.

Philippine Census. 1960. *Census of the Philippines, 1960.* Manila: Bureau of Census and Statistics.

PNSO. 2008. *Population and Demography.* Philippine National Statistics Office. Manila: Office of National Statistics. http://www.census.gov.ph/.

Popkin, Samuel L. 1979. *The Rational Peasant: The Political Economy of Rural Society in Vietnam.* Berkeley: University of California Press.

Powdermaker, Hortense. 1966. *Stranger and Friend: The Way of an Anthropologist.* New York and London: W. W. Norton.

Radin, Paul. 1920. *The Autobiography of a Winnebago Indian.* University of California Publications in American Archaeology and Ethnology, 16(7):381–473. http://archive.org/stream/autobiowinne00blowrich#page/n3/mode/2up.

Rappaport, Roy A. 2000[1984]. *Pigs for the Ancestors: Ritual of the Ecology of a New Guinea People.* 2nd ed. Long Grove, IL: Waveland Press.

Redfield, Robert. 1930. *Tepotzlan, a Mexican Village: A Study in Folk Life.* Chicago: University of Chicago Press.

Reed, Robert R. 1963. "Corn." In *Shadows on the Land.* Robert E. Huke, ed. Pp. 242–267. Makati, Philippines: Carmelo & Bauermann.

Republic of the Philippines. 1997. Republic Act No. 8371. The Indigenous Peoples Rights Act of 1997. The LawPhil Project. http://www.lawphil.net/statutes/repacts/ra1997/ra_8371_1997.html.

Rideout, Henry M. 1912. *William Jones: Indian, Cowboy, American Scholar, and Anthropologist in the Field.* New York: Frederick A. Stokes.

Rigdon, Susan M. 1988. *The Culture Facade. Art, Science, and Politics in the Work of Oscar Lewis.* Urbana: University of Illinois Press.

Roberts, John M., R. F. Strand, and E. Burmeister. 1971. "Preferential Pattern Analysis." In *Explorations in Mathematical Anthropology.* Paul Kay, ed. Pp. 242–268. Cambridge: MIT Press.

Robertson, Jennifer. 2002. "Reflexivity Redux: A Pithy Polemic on 'Positionality.'" *Anthropological Quarterly* 75(4):785–792.

Romney, A. Kimball, and C. C. Moore. 1998. "Toward a Theory of Culture as Shared Cognitive Structures." *Ethos* 126:314–337.

Rosaldo, Michelle. 1980. *Knowledge and Passion: Ilongot Notions of Self and Social Life.* New York: Cambridge University Press.

Rosaldo, Renato. 1980. *Ilongot Headhunting: 1883–1974.* Palo Alto, CA: Stanford University Press.

Royce, Anya Peterson, and Robert V. Kemper. 2002. "Long-Term Field Research: Metaphors, Paradigms, and Themes." In *Chronicling Cultures: Long-Term Field Research in Anthropology.* Robert V. Kemper and Anya Peterson Royce, eds. Pp. xiv–xxxviii. Walnut Creek, CA: Altamira Press.

Salzman, Philip C. 2002. "On Reflexivity." *American Anthropologist* 104(3):805–813.

Sanga, Glauco, and Gherado Ortalli, eds. 2004. *Nature Knowledge: Ethnoscience, Cognition, and Utility.* Oxford: Berghahn Books.

Sanjek, Roger. 1991. "The Ethnographic Present." *Man* 26(4):609–628.

Scheper-Hughes, Nancy. 2001. *Saints, Scholars, and Schizophrenics: Mental Illness in Rural Ireland.* Twentieth Anniversary Edition, Updated and Expanded. Berkeley, Los Angeles, London: University of California Press.

Schusky, Ernest L., and Fred Eggan 1989. "Fred Eggan: Anthropologist Full Circle." *American Ethnologist* 16(1):142–157.

Scott, William Henry. 1992. *Looking for Prehispanic Filipino and Other Essays in Philippine History.* Quezon City, Philippines: New Day.

Sears, Paul. 1939. *Life and Environment: The Interrelation of Living Things.* Bureau of Publications, Teachers College, Columbia University.

Service, Elman R. 1958. *A Profile of Primitive Culture.* New York: Harper & Row.

Soderstrom, Mark. 2004. "Family Trees and Timber Rights: Albert E. Jenks, Americanization, and the Rise of Anthropology at the University of Minnesota." *Journal of the Gilded Age and Progressive Era* 3(2):176–204.

Spradley, James P. 1972. *Culture and Cognition: Rules, Maps and Plans.* San Francisco: Chandler.

———. 1979. *The Ethnographic Interview.* New York: Holt, Rinehart and Winston.

Spencer, J. E. 1966. *Shifting Cultivation in Southeast Asia.* University of California Publication in Geography, vol. 19. Berkeley, Los Angeles, London: University of California Press.

Spiro, Melford E. 1996. "Postmodernist Anthropology, Subjectivity, and Science: A Modern Critique." *Comparative Studies in Society and History* 38(4):759–780.

Steward, Julian. 1936. *Pueblo Material Culture in Western Utah.* Anthropological Series, 1(3), University of New Mexico Bulletin No. 287, 1–64. Albuquerque: University of New Mexico.

Swadesh, Morris. 1950. "Salish Internal Relationships." *International Journal of American Linguistics* 16:157–167.

———. 1955. "Towards Greater Accuracy in Lexicostatistic Dating," *International Journal of American Linguistics* 21:121–137.

———. 1971. *The Origin and Diversification of Language.* Chicago: Aldine. (Edited postmortem by Joel Sherzer.)

Tuzin, Donald. 1997. *The Cassowary's Revenge: The Life and Death of Masculinity in a New Guinea Society.* Chicago: University of Chicago Press.

Tyler, Stephen A. 1969. *Cognitive Anthropology.* New York: Holt, Rinehart and Winston.

Umali, D. L. 1960. *A Student Manuel for Use in Vocational Agriculture.* Laguna: University of the Philippines, College of Agriculture.

Van den Top, Gerhard. 2003. *The Social Dynamics of Deforestation in the Philippines: Actions, Options and Motivations.* Copenhagen: Nordic Institute of Asian Studies, Man and Nature in Asia Series, No. 6.

Veenhoven, Ruut. 2006. "Quality of Life in Modern Society Measured with Happy Life Years." In *Happiness and Public Policy: Theory, Case Studies and Implications.* Yew-Kwang Ng and Lok Sang Ho, eds. Pp. 19–44. New York: Palgrave Macmillan.

———. 2010. "Life Is Getting Better: Societal Evolution and Fit with Human Nature." *Social Indicators Research* 97:105–122.

Wallace, Ben J. 1964. *The Oklahoma Kickapoo: An Ethnographic Reconstruction.* Milwaukee: Wisconsin Archaeologist No. 45.

———. 1969. *Shifting Cultivation and Plow Agriculture in Two Pagan Gaddang Settlements.* Manila: Institute of Science and Technology Monograph No. 11.

———. 1970. *Hill and Valley Farmers: Socio-Economic Change Among a Philippine People.* Cambridge: Schenkman.

———. 1975. "Pagan Gaddang Mediums." *Arctic Anthropology,* Festschrift issue in honor of Chester S. Chard: 11:204–212.

———. 1983. "Plants, Pigs, and People: Studying the Food Web in Pagan Gaddang." *Ethnology* 22(1):27–41.

————. 1987. *The Invisible Resource: Women and Work in Rural Bangladesh.* Boulder, CO and London: Westview Press.

————. 2006. *The Changing Village Life in Southeast Asia: Applied Anthropology and Environment in the Northern Philippines.* New York and London: RoutledgeCurzon.

————. 2009. "Critical Reflections: Confessions from the Director of a Fifteen-Year Agroforestry Project in the Philippines." *Human Organization* 68(1):55–64.

Weiner, Annette. 1976. *Women of Value, Men of Renown: New Perspectives in Trobriand Exchange.* Austin: University of Texas Press.

Wernstedt, F. L., and J. E. Spencer. 1967. *The Philippine Island World: A Physical, Cultural, and Regional Geography.* Berkeley: University of California Press.

Wilson, Monica. 1970. *Good Company: A Study of Nyakyusa Age-Village.* Boston: Beacon Press.

Whiteford, Linda M., and Robert T. Trotter II. 2008. *Ethics for Anthropological Research and Practice.* Long Grove, IL: Waveland Press.

Wolf, Margery. 1992. *A Thrice Told Tale: Feminism, Postmodernism & Ethnographic Responsibility.* Palo Alto, CA: Stanford University Press.

Wolfe, Thomas. 1934. *You Can't Go Home Again.* New York: Harper & Row.

Yengoyan, Aram A., and Perla Q. Makil, eds. 1984. *Selected Essay of Frank Lynch: Philippine Society and the Individual.* Quezon City, Philippines: Ateneo de Manila.

Yorobe, Jose M., and Cesar B. Quicoy. 2006. "Economic Impact of Bt Corn in the Philippines." *The Philippine Agricultural Scientist* 89(3):258–267.

Zamora, Mario D. 1974. "Henry Otley Beyer, 1883–1966." *American Anthropologist* 76(2):361–362.

————. 1986. "Robert Bradford Fox, 1918–1985." *The Journal of Asian Studies* 45(3):667.

Zeitlyn, David. 2009. "Understanding Anthropological Understanding: For a Merological Anthropology." *Anthropological Theory* 9(2):209–231.